GLOBETROTTER

Travel

NEW YORK CITY

MICHAEL LEECH

NEW
HOLLAND

This edition first published in 2001
by New Holland Publishers (UK) Ltd
London • Cape Town • Sydney • Auckland
First published in 1997
10 9 8 7 6 5 4 3 2 1

Garfield House, 86 Edgware Road
London W2 2EA
United Kingdom

80 McKenzie Street
Cape Town 8001
South Africa

14 Aquatic Drive
Frenchs Forest NSW2086
Australia

218 Lake Road, Northcote
Auckland
New Zealand

Distributed in the USA by
The Globe Pequot Press
Connecticut

ISBN 1 85974 815 5

Manager Globetrotter Maps: John Loubser
Managing Editor: Thea Grobbelaar
Editors: Susannah Coucher, Anna Bennett
Picture Researcher: Jan Croot
Design and DTP: Sonya Cupido

Consultant: Paul Barnett
Cartographer: Renée Barnes
Compiler/Verifier: Elaine Fick
Reproduction by Hirt & Carter (Pty) Ltd, Cape Town
Printed and bound in Hong Kong by Sing Cheong
Printing Co. Ltd.

Cover: *The Brooklyn Bridge, Lower Manhattan.*
Title Page: *The famous skyline from a cruise boat.*

CONTENTS

1. Introducing New York City 5
The Land 6
History in Brief 11
Government and Economy 18
The People 20

2. Lower Manhattan 31
The Best of Lower Manhattan 32
Other Museums and
Places of Interest 34
The Civic Center and
South Street Seaport 36

**3. Lower East Side
and East Village 39**
Lower East Side 40
East Village 45

**4. Greenwich Village,
SoHo and TriBeCa 49**
Greenwich Village 50
SoHo 54
TriBeCa 56

**5. Chelsea and
Gramercy Park 59**
Sights to See 60
Old Residential Districts 62

6. Midtown 65
The Garment District 66
Shopping Along West 34th Street 68
Murray Hill and East 42nd Street 70
Fifth Avenue – West Side 73
Fifth Avenue – East Side 78

7. Upper East Side 81
Central Park 82
Museums 84

8. Upper West Side 89
Cultural Venues 90
Walking on the West Side 92

**9. Harlem and Washington
Heights 95**
Around 125th Street 96
Washington Heights 99

10. Beyond Manhattan 101
Brooklyn and Queens 102
The Bronx and Staten Island 104
Long Island 106
Beaches 107
New Jersey 108
Connecticut 110
Lower New York State 111

New York City at a Glance 113

Travel Tips 122

Index 127

1
Introducing New York City

New York is one of those towns that must be seen by sophisticated travellers. Smart, sharp and sweet, New York is always fascinating. This very exciting city incorporates both the best and liveliest of the American Experience and is always awake. For the dedicated night-bird there's no place like **Manhattan**; equally, for those not intrigued by nightclubs, cabarets or bizarre theatrical events, there is an enormous variety of things to do by day. It's the ultimate urban experience: a place to set the heart and senses racing.

New York City isn't simple: it's composed of five boroughs but most visitors venture no further than mighty Manhattan. But consider visits to **Brooklyn**, **Queens**, even the **Bronx**, which has a fantastic botanical garden. A ferry ride over the Hudson to **Staten Island** (actually the fifth borough of Richmond) is one of those great experiences as you take in the **Statue of Liberty**, welcoming you to her towered city on the waves. Unofficially New York also incorporates chunks of nearby New Jersey, the city's suburbs in New York State (one of the biggest in the union) and what you might call NYC country: the rural stretches of northern **New Jersey** and **Long Island**. New Yorkers migrate en masse to small towns and beach resorts in the high heat of summer, transforming places like Easthampton, Fire Island and Amagansett into the city in the country.

Although not a capital, New York has attracted many to its social meltdown. It's a wonderful mixture, and for the sophisticated New Yorker there is just no place like it.

Top Attractions

*** **Midtown:** Broadway and some fabulous shops.
*** **World-Class Buildings:** the Empire State, the Seagram, the Chrysler and the World Trade buildings.
** **Top Shops:** on Fifth Avenue and 34th Street.
** **Central Park:** Manhattan's great green oasis.
** **Greenwich Village and SoHo:** neighbourhoods where art is king.
* **Lincoln Center:** grand opera, dance and drama in one splendid location.
* **Manhattan Cruise:** magnificent views from the water.

Opposite: *A sea-gull's view of the business heart of Manhattan.*

Above: *An inkling of how Manhattan used to be can be gained from its major public parks.*
Opposite: *Construction is ever a facet of New York City and jack hammers and steam vents add to the hubbub.*

THE LAND

Three hundred years ago Manhattan was merely a rocky platform above a well-protected harbour opening to the East River and the Hudson. The waterways are still there but Manhattan has totally changed. To begin with, it has been flattened out and most of its hills removed. To gain an impression of the original geography of the island, walk through **Central Park**, where in parts there is still a certain natural 'feel' of age-old land. Despite the park's overall design with modern paths and roads, huge rocks still thrust up through the terrain, and many of the trees (such as maple) and plants are indigenous.

The rocky foundation of the island meant secure footings for big buildings, and now Manhattan is crowned with the modern equivalent of medieval castles, an impressive and rightly famous parade of steel, glass and concrete towers. The renowned skyline is a riveting sight, especially when you consider that a few decades ago there would have been no tall buildings at all. Major upward expansion began early in the 20th century and has been pushing up vertically ever since. New York's buildings created a new word for a world that, except for Gothic cathedrals, had been up to that time low-rise: skyscraper. Asia now challenges for 'world's tallest buildings' yet New York still has some of the most dramatic constructions the world has ever seen.

The Island between the Rivers

The rivers to the east and west of Manhattan are natural dividing lines. The **Hudson River** marks the border of New York City and is also the state line between New Jersey and New York. Even so, these settlements are really suburbs of New York that happen to be in another state.

The **East River**, a short waterway from harbour to sea, essentially an inlet with Long Island as its eastern shore, divides Manhattan from Brooklyn and Queens, while the harbour into which both rivers feed is the

NEW YORK CITY	J	F	M	A	M	J	J	A	S	O	N	D
AVERAGE TEMP. °C	0	1	5	11	17	22	25	24	20	15	8	2
AVERAGE TEMP. °F	32	33	41	52	62	71	77	75	68	58	47	36
Hours of sun daily	2	3	4	6	7	8	9	8	7	4	3	2
Days of rainfall	12	10	12	11	11	10	12	10	9	9	9	10
RAINFALL mm	94	97	91	81	81	84	107	109	86	89	76	91
RAINFALL in	4	4	4	3.5	3.5	3.5	4	4	3.5	3.5	3	4

division for Staten Island. The East River also forms the narrow channel between Manhattan and the Bronx, becoming the **Harlem River** running off the Hudson. Every effort has been made to clean up the Harlem River but it is an ongoing problem.

Climate
The city essentially has two climates: hot and cold. It's snowy, windy and very cold and frosty in winter, but with a dry, healthy chill that makes for brisk walks and skating in Central Park or in the Rockefeller Center rink. In the sweaty humidity of high summer everyone retreats to air-conditioned offices and apartments if possible. Between these two extremes are brief cool periods of spring and the fall, or autumn which is often characterized with lovely, warm days and clear skies. New York skies are often cloudless and a brilliant blue.

THE HUDSON RIVER

The Hudson is a beautiful river, starting in the **Adirondack Mountains**. At its southern end it widens and is the border between NY State and New Jersey. Early residents recall the Hudson as being full of fish, and a great occasion was the annual run of the shad, with the delicious shad roe a pop- ular dish in spring. The valley has varied scenery and old riverside buildings to explore on days out from the city.

Plant Life
Some of the city streets are tree-lined, especially in residential areas, but trees and shrubs need to be resistant to New York's pollution. Many residents fill window sills and flat roofs with tubs and pots. It is certainly worth a trip out to Brooklyn in order to see the specialist collections. Or, alternatively, you could combine a trip to the Bronx and the New York Botanical Garden which has large gardens and native plants, with the well-kept Bronx Zoo.

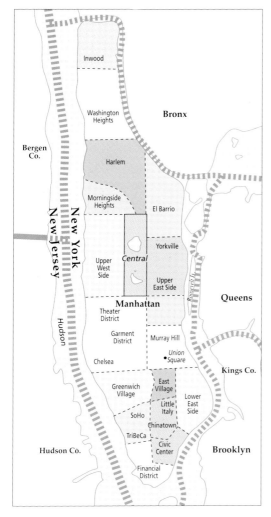

Wildlife

Even in the concrete city there is a concern for wildlife. Nest boxes are fixed to office walls for peregrine falcons (they prey on the pigeons, which are pests). Central Park contains rare plants, trees and flowers and in the International Wildlife Conservation Center, you will see some 764 species in their habitats.

City Profile

The forming of five boroughs of such disparate size and style appears to have been fairly arbitrary. New York seems to have just grown, without much planning, to what it is now, and is still changing constantly. Yet that is a vital part of what the city is all about and New Yorkers are quite used to roads being dug up, sidewalks cut off, and whole buildings coming down almost overnight. Buildings are replaced almost as quickly, sometimes with ugly 'egg boxes', but often with creations of surprising style. However, you can still find elements of old New York if you search, and it's a rewarding aspect in this ever-modernizing city to find here and there evocative little left-behind bits of another age.

New York originated at its southern tip with the first buildings erected by Dutch settlers in the early 17th century. None of these Colonial buildings exist now but the pattern of streets still shows us what went before: the reason Broadway angles so conspicuously across the island is because originally it was an ancient Indian track.

Contemporary streetplans indicate a settlement which slowly began to develop in the 18th and 19th centuries until in 1811 the Randel Plan was put into effect, mapping out future development of the island according to a **grid system**, with long avenues going north and crossing with narrower east–west streets. This plan goes from 14th Street. Broadway angles right across it; the Financial District is narrower; Greenwich Village streets can puzzle.

Starting in the south, explore the **Battery** and the harbour front. An area which was once renowned for its rowdiness, it is now an international business district and the city's **financial** and **government centre**. **Wall Street's** name comes from the first years of the city when it was the street next to the northernmost stockade wall of the burgeoning village. This wall was there to keep the Algonquin Indians out.

Above: *The Trump Tower on Fifth Avenue is a slice of glass angled to the street.*
Below: *St Mark's Place is a lively and very real part of the city.*

Above: *It may seem confusing, yet signs are clear, routes direct.*

Pressing close are **SoHo** and **TriBeCa**, renovated areas, and now fashionable places for art galleries and studios, then **Greenwich Village** and **Chelsea** followed by **Midtown** and the theatres of **Broadway**. Department stores and airline offices cluster on this part of **Fifth Avenue**. The green spread of **Central Park** divides the **Upper East** and the **Upper West Sides**; at the northern line of the park **Harlem** begins, then **Washington Heights**.

The **boroughs** beyond grew as Manhattan enlarged and needed more workers: they are typical **sleeper suburbs** (where many New York workers reside) with many small independent (detached and split-level) houses, all part of the larger New York, but it's worth remembering that, before its incorporation as a borough in 1898, **Brooklyn** was a separate and prosperous city. The boroughs are cut up with major highways, often elevated, and with main roads curving off in every direction.

New York is necklaced with fast highways, many bridges and tunnels, and in theory it ought to be easy to get around but traffic jams abound at certain times. The continuous unrelenting pressure of traffic, particularly heavy delivery vehicles, is hard on the streets. In addition, penetrating winter frosts literally break up the avenues, causing large and rather dangerous pot holes in the spring through which the yellow taxi cabs lurch.

GROWING OLDER

Even though buildings such as the **Empire State** and the **Woolworth** have the prestige of being classic buildings or historic landmarks, other less well-known ones are faced with a dilemma. A problem with older buildings is that as they age and business-people demand gleaming new accommodation, they become difficult to rent. Maybe NYC should follow Philadelphia's example with its Avenue of the Arts, which is a commendable attempt at recycling and finding new uses for these 'antique buildings'.

HISTORY IN BRIEF

Early Settlers

The history of the city begins with the early explorers, who arrived from the 16th century onwards, but little attempt was made to settle until the **Dutch** established a permanent trading post in 1624 which became known as **Nieuw (New) Amsterdam**. There is an ancient tale about Manhattan being purchased from the Native Indians at a bargain price by Peter Minuit, the Director of the Dutch West Indies Company, in 1626. These original settlers (then called Red Indians) had infiltrated from Asia across the Bering Sea millennia ago, and the **Algonquin** tribes had spread along the east coast of the new continent. They reportedly received strings of beads and some gaudy trinkets worth 60 guilders in exchange for their land rights from the thrifty Netherlanders. Whether it is true or not, the original residents called the land 'Manahatta', an Algonquian word probably meaning 'island of the hills'.

The Dutch set about with typical ingenuity to make the hostile island livable, digging canals, smoothing out hills and filling in the shoreline. They beavered away for half a century but New Amsterdam wasn't destined to last

'PEG LEG PETE'

The Dutch provided hard work and direction, and a few colourful characters. Notable was Peter Stuyvesant, drafted in from Holland in 1647 as governor to organize a colony that had become lawless and unruly. A stern Calvinist, he curtailed drinking hours in the taverns and came down heavily on freethinkers and Quakers. Not surprising then that the settlers, who had had things to themselves until his arrival, resented his rigid rule. They would not have been able to comprehend how 'Peg Leg Pete' (so-called on account of his wooden leg) has become a legend, his name labelling institutions and schools.

Left: *In this contemporary etching you get an idea of the tough, arrogant man who was Peter Stuyvesant.*

WILLIAM 'BOSS' TWEED

Not surprisingly the expanding new city was riddled with corruption. In the 1860s William 'Boss' Tweed took command and headed **Tammany Hall,** building up a political organization which soon became synonymous with greed. His rule engulfed city government; Tweed and his cronies milked the city of millions of dollars until he was exposed by the *New York Times* in 1871.

Opposite: *Yet another building will rise as the wrecker's ball destroys old neighbourhoods.*
Below: *The nation's first President and native son, George Washington.*

as a Dutch settlement. **Britain** was eager to increase her overseas possessions, and in 1664, at a time when the British and Dutch were involved in ferocious trade wars, Charles II gave the colony to his brother, the Duke of York. British warships blockaded New York harbour and took the city without firing a single shot. New Amsterdam was then renamed New York.

New York prospered under British rule. The first newspaper, the *New York Gazette*, was established in 1725; in 1754 Columbia University (then called King's) was founded. With its harbour as a prime possession, trade by sea developed constantly. From small beginnings, by the mid-18th century the city had become a major port, and on the eve of the Revolution it was the second largest city in the colonies with 20,000 citizens.

The city was strategically vital during the **War of Independence** (1776–83) and after various skirmishes with Washington's troops, New York was held by the British for the duration. However, the colonies eventually won their freedom and the British were forced to concede control of the city.

Although it had kept a low wartime profile, New York was briefly the new nation's capital (1785–90) to be followed by Philadelphia (1790-1800). In 1789 **George Washington** was inaugurated as President of the United States in New York's new Federal Hall. Around this time the city developed an infant financial infrastructure by opening the first bank and a stock exchange, thus laying the foundations for its role as a world financial centre.

The Making of the Metropolis

As Manhattan flowed relentlessly north, hemmed in by its two rivers, it developed a series of defined districts. Inevitably many of these have changed, some beyond all recognition – for this was originally an island of small farms. It may be hard to imagine now, especially as these rural settlements have become the Financial District. The Lower East Side is no longer the same place where waves of 19th-century immigrants settled in overcrowded tenement buildings, and Midtown has few of its original distinctive brownstone row houses.

As the nation's premier seaport in a new, aggressive nation, New York became increasingly wealthy. In 1811 the city governors came up with the **Randel Plan**, a grid system that catered for future expansion by laying out New York in over 2000 rectangular blocks.

Despite the British blockade of New York harbour in the War of 1812, the city continued to prosper. The opening of the **Erie Canal** in 1825 gave the east coast access to trade with the US interior and the Canadian lakes. By the middle of the century, New York was the most prosperous city in the country; traders and industrial tycoons were making fortunes. Manufacturing increased and the rich moved uptown.

PROHIBITION

As alcohol was denied under legislation in 1919, so illegal drinking of 'bathtub gin' and other home-made liquors grew and crime prospered in the new lucrative market. Speakeasies (drinking dens) flourished all over New York. It was fashionable for the wealthy to go up to Harlem to the Cotton Club to dance, drink and drug, to hear the new jazz and see the black stars emerging from that vital hotspot. The way that most poor Harlem residents lived was totally unknown to most well-off New Yorkers, but it was smart and life was fast and exhilarating.

Immigration

In the 19th century immigration rolled in like a tide, and New York was the main receiving point for settlers from Europe. The new arrivals came by sea, often after a fearful crossing. Africans were brought in to the southern ports of the United States as slaves. Many moved north to find a free life and in New York they headed for the borough of Harlem.

Between 1840–57, three million Irish and Germans arrived in New York harbour. Most fanned out across America to create a new nation, though many stayed in

---

HISTORICAL CALENDAR

?BC–16th century Land occupied by groups of Algonquin Indians.
1524 Giovanni da Verrazano sails into New York harbour.
1609 Henry Hudson, working for the Dutch, arrives in New York Bay.
1624 The Dutch establish first trading post.
1626 Peter Minuit buys Manhattan for a few trinkets.
1647 Peter Stuyvesant becomes governor.
1664 The British snatch the colony and change its name to New York.
1776 War of Independence begins.
1783 USA wins independence; British evacuate New York.
1785–90 New York is USA capital.
1812–14 British blockade New York harbour.
1825 Erie Canal opens.
1835 Fire razes much of city to ground.
1858 Central Park designed.
1861–5 American Civil War.
1868 First elevated railroad built on Greenwich Street.
1883 Brooklyn Bridge completed.
1886 Statue of Liberty unveiled.
1892 Cathedral of St John the Divine begun; Ellis Island opens.
1909 Wilbur Wright flies first plane

over New York.
1911 Triangle Shirtwaist Factory fire kills 146 sweatshop workers; New York Public Library completed.
1919 18th Amendment bans alcohol and launches Prohibition.
1929 Stock Market Crash followed by the Great Depression.
1931 Empire State becomes world's tallest building.
1933 Prohibition ends; Fiorello LaGuardia becomes mayor.
1941–45 USA involved in World War II.
1946 UN establishes HQ in New York.
1948 Idlewild Airport opens. Now JFK.
1954 Ellis Island closes.
1962 Avery Fisher Hall, first building in Lincoln Center, completed.
1973 World Trade Center completed.
1976 Statue of Liberty restored for her 100th year.
1980–90 Near bankruptcy then boom.
1990s 42nd Street clean up.
1994 Mayor Guiliani elected on a clean up New York City programme.
1996 Victory Theater re-opened.
2000 Hilary Clinton elected New York State Senator.

the city. New York was unprepared for such an influx: fires, epidemics, overcrowding and fearful poverty ensued. The gap between rich and poor widened; there were riots and looting.

After the Civil War, New York embarked on a grand scale of civic building. Central Park was created in 1858; a range of apartment blocks, hotels and department stores were built and railways – both national and local – were developed. In 1880 the Metropolitan Museum of Art opened; around the same time the New York Public Library and Carnegie Hall were founded. The landmark Brooklyn Bridge was completed in 1883.

From 1870 onwards a new wave of Italian, east European and Chinese immigrants came to New York. Ellis Island opened in 1892 to facilitate their entry. At the turn of the century, the population density of the Lower East Side (where most of the immigrants lived) was 330,000 per sq mile, the highest in the world. Living and working conditions were appalling. Tenement buildings were unhygienic and overcrowded. People toiled long hours for a pittance in dangerous sweatshops. Working conditions didn't improve until after the Triangle Shirtwaist Factory fire in 1911, when 146 young women working in a sweatshop were burned to death. Tougher laws and fire escapes were then implemented.

ALGONQUIN ROUND TABLE

Renowned for her smart quips ('you can lead a whore to culture but you cannot make her think'), **Dorothy Parker** was a queen among the wordsharps who met at the Algonquin Hotel, just over the road from the *New Yorker* offices. She and other wits held up a mirror to the times, and gave New York much of the image it preserves today as a centre of smart repartee, humorous verse and quick cracks. Alas, the Algonquin (on West 43rd Street) hasn't resounded with such hilarity for decades, but writers, agents and publishers still meet there and you can visit, have tea or a drink in its foyer, and enjoy its unique clubby atmosphere. You can even dine at the famous Round Table installed for the benefit of Parker and her cohorts.

Left: *View of the ever-growing city from the splendid viewpoint of Brooklyn Bridge.*
Opposite: *The Immigration Halls on Ellis Island, where for a century new arrivals were processed, are now a museum.*

One of New York's best known, and more rarely, best loved mayors, was **Fiorello LaGuardia**, who was voted into office in 1933 and served until 1945. The 'Little Flower' worked hard to give back to New York a renewed sense of self-respect and optimism. He inaugurated many projects to keep citizens in work, and also gained funding for the poor through Federal aid. He's still affectionately remembered and LaGuardia Airport, opened in 1939, is named after him.

Between the Wars

The United States played a considerable part in the realigning of Europe when wartime chaos ended in 1918. It then entered into a frenetic time of expansion and money-making in the 1920s. This was reflected mostly in the big cities which became like magnets to anyone who wanted to feel they were in the centre of things. The biggest magnet of all was New York.

Picture files of the period bulge with shots of the fashionable and famous descending from ocean liners along the Hudson River Docks. Film stars, fashion designers, fast-living aristocrats and the new business tycoons, as well as famous names from Noël Coward to Gertrude Stein, arrived and were swept up by the excitement. The theatre boomed, although the fledgling film industry had already moved to California, where the sun was more certain. Skyscrapers rocketed up; foundations were laid for the Chrysler Building, the Empire State and the Rockefeller Center.

The 1920s were a time of growth and high living, epitomized by New York's flamboyant mayor, Jimmy Walker. Alcohol was outlawed but speakeasies flourished. The economic boom began to spiral out of control and confidence in the stock market came to an abrupt end

Below: *Soaring up against summer skies, the Chrysler was the tallest building in the world for about a year.*

with the Wall Street Crash in October 1929. By 1932 Walker had resigned amid accusations of corruption. More than a quarter of New Yorkers were out of work and thousands lived in shantytowns known as 'Hoovervilles' (after the president). The USA was in the grip of the terrible **Great Depression**. This continued right up until the mid-1930s and was only alleviated by radical government intervention.

Left: *An impressive parade of the flags of the members represented at the United Nations.*

In New York the WPA or Works Progress Administration was greatly responsible for the city's economic recovery, creating thousands of jobs and encouraging projects from construction to artworks.

Post-War New York

A new mood prevailed after 1945 and the accent was on growth again. The United Nations established its headquarters here in 1946, a major coup for the city. Idlewild Airport (renamed John F. Kennedy Airport after the president's assasination in 1963) was opened in 1948 to encourage more business. The huge flood of immigrants had greatly slowed down so in 1954 Ellis Island processed its last New American. New York continued to tear down and re-erect buildings, with new projects including the Lever Building, the Seagram and the Lincoln Center. The Financial District was especially subject to rebuilding, and the World Trade Towers were completed in 1976.

Recent decades witnessed racial strife, crime and violence, now coming under control. The city almost went bankrupt in the 1970s but experienced an economic boom in the 1980s, which has now tailed off. Vast areas of Manhattan have been regenerated and gentrified, but there is a marked polarity between rich and poor.

THE WALL STREET CRASH

Although there had been financial warnings and tremors the Crash was not expected and everyone was encouraged to gamble. Huge sums were being made on the Stock Market and this paved the way for a dreadful and shocking fall in October 1929 that paralyzed not only the United States but the rest of the world. It resulted in the Depression and New Yorkers suffered as much as the rest of the country. Strangely enough, there was some growth during this period – such as civil projects which included the construction of the city's skyscrapers.

GOVERNMENT AND ECONOMY

The Mayor of New York is no mere figurehead: he (or maybe one day she) is a very powerful political force, as epitomized by Mayor Fiorello LaGuardia or, more recently, Rudolph Giuliani. In 1989 New York's government was reformed and now it is a 35-member city council. Each of the five boroughs has a certain amount of independence of legislation.

New York has always been a boom-and-bust town, and it continues to lurch from crisis to crisis in government, with few people believing in the evergreen promises of politicians. Things came to a head in the 1970s after a period of unrest in the previous decade, when riots were witnessed in Harlem after the terrible assassinations of the era, notably of President Kennedy and the Reverend Martin Luther King.

In the mid-1970s came the announcement that New York was virtually bankrupt. Ed Koch was elected mayor and his emergency moves effected a revival of business and construction. Inevitably this was followed by a period of uncertainty with the Gulf War and a recession in the 1990s. Ed Koch lost his job in 1989, and his replacement, New York's first black mayor, David Dinkins, elected on a platform of continuing growth, moved over for Mayor Giuliani in 1992. Giuliani's Zero Tolerance policy has dramatically reduced crime rates in the city.

Although poverty and crime are still very evident in some quarters, with the lack of jobs being a major problem particularly for disadvantaged youth, somehow the city manages to pull through. New Yorkers are a tough breed, and they love their city, warts and all. They continue to support the dream that there is such a state as a healthy and financially balanced city, beliefs which instill strength and confidence in the populace. As its citizens go on, so does New York.

MANHATTAN FACT FILE

Population: 7.4 million.
Area: 13.4 miles (21.5km) long; 2.3 miles (3.7km) wide.
Taxis: 12,000.
Art galleries: there are about 500 galleries.
Skyscrapers: there are about 200 skyscrapers.
Broadway theatres: there are 40 recognized Broadway theatres.
Lower Manhattan: 30% is built on reclaimed land created by landfills.
Empire State Building: visibility from the 102nd floor on a clear day is an amazing 80 miles (129km).
'Big Apple': a term coined in the 1920s by jazz musicians as a way of saying 'There are many apples on the tree, but when you pick New York City, you pick the Big Apple.'

Economic Development

A fact that makes many non-New Yorkers envious is that New York is first in so many fields. The number one city in the United States, it is also the biggest conference and incentive meeting place in the country. It's the major **business** and **financial** centre, with the number one stock exchanges. Although trade by sea has fallen away, it still acts as a major port and its three airports handle cargoes from around the world. **Industry** is a giant and there's a big construction business, and constant encouraging of new companies to come and set up, particularly in the outer boroughs beyond Manhattan. **Fashion** and the garment industry are big employers. **Tourism** is a major money-winner bringing billions to the city each year. As such, the city has developed both the infrastructure and the attractions, making it the most exciting visitor destination in the world. The theatre and **entertainment** industries, volatile though they are, flourish and encourage a whole growth of other industries from taxi services and parking lots to hotels and restaurants. The **arts** are big money here – major auction houses flourish and there is more book-publishing than anywhere else in the country.

FIFTH AVENUE

A name that still resounds with glamour, this long avenue goes all the way from the **Washington Arch** below 8th Street to 125th Street in Harlem. It gives a view of the city as it changes dramatically, from the casual air of **Greenwich Village** to smart **Midtown**. An almost country-like stretch edges the park in the wealthy **Upper East Side** to a rundown end beyond 110th Street in **Spanish Harlem**. It is the spine of the city, dividing East and West, and many famous buildings stand along it.

Above: *Street signs plaster poles on the corners and they can be confusing.*
Left: *The World Trade Center's blocks frame a plaza and monumental sculpture.*
Opposite: *President Kennedy was not a New Yorker but he and his wife maintained a residence there.*

NEW YORK HUMOUR

Like all great cities, from London to Berlin and Paris to Sydney, New York has its own decided sense of humour. It probably started with the immigrants, who had to be cheerful to keep going. New York certainly has roots with Jewish comedians of Yiddish theatres of the Lower East Side, and New York continues to take in new forms as new residents arrive. This type of humour continues to inspire many New Yorkers, especially in today's tough times.

THE PEOPLE

New York City has flattened out in terms of population growth and, like London, now maintains a figure of above 7 million. These two cities, having long claimed to be the biggest in the world, are now far smaller than **São Paulo** in Brazil and **Mexico City**. Yet New York has always been diverse, always received the mass of new citizens, and it remains a mixture of many races. This is very evident from your first trip on the subway!

Over half of the population is white, about one-quarter is black, and there is a large sprinkling of Asians as well as Native Americans. There's really no ethnic majority, but a number of minorities. **Hispanics** are now the most numerous in this grouping.

Of the original European settler groups, many still live in New York and, while not as numerous as they once were, the **Irish**, **Italian** and **Jewish** citizens do still make a vital and concerned contribution to city life and government. This is sometimes evident in specific areas: at one time half of the New York police force seemed to be Irish. More recent arrivals have been from the **Caribbean** (especially Puerto Rico and Haiti) and a considerable influx has also been received from **Russia**, **Central America**, **India** and **Southeast Asia**. New arrivals tend to group together. For example, you'll find many fruit and vegetable stands run by **Vietnamese** and **Koreans** on the Lower East Side.

Below: *Buskers in Manhattan do all sorts of tricks to attract the crowds.*

Language

Although to all intents English is the first language, Americans sometimes use different words to mean different things. You will find an example of these Americanisms on p. 123. Although you will have no difficulty in being understood in New York,

Spanish has unmistakably
made its mark and is a growing language. Signs on shops,
boardings, subways and
buses are catering more
and more for Hispanics. The
Spanish-speaking citizens,
who are mostly from Puerto
Rico, Cuba and South and
Central America, have
brought a new mixture
and lively presence to
this ever-changing city.

Above: *A renewed police
presence in New York
helps to make the visitors
feel more confident.*

   Apart from these two languages, there are many
others to be heard as you walk around the principal
streets. **Yiddish** was once prevalent, although less
frequently heard now. **Greek**, **Italian**, **Russian** and
Turkish have their own areas, and in Chinatown you
can hear not one but several of the **Chinese** tongues.

Religion

Religions run the gamut of world beliefs, alongside all
kinds of cults. Although long ago the established religion
was essentially Protestant in its many forms, Catholicism is
a big force, established by the immigrants from Ireland and
Italy. New York's two most famous churches are
St John the Divine and **St Patrick's**. There are many synagogues, mosques and temples. Whatever your belief,
you will find some element of it in this city.

Festivals and Parades

There's hardly a week that goes by without some form of
parade or celebration and these events tend to be big, gregarious and great fun. The **Columbus Day Parade** draws
huge crowds. Whole areas may be transformed, whether
they are for local festivals or big events. On **St Patrick's
Day**, Fifth Avenue and even the flowers in their stands
are coloured green, and the parade is received by dignit-
aries on the steps of St Patrick's Cathedral; and the locals
of the Lower East Side celebrate the **Ukrainian Festival** in

---

NEW YORK'S
FIRST ST PATRICK'S

St Patrick's Cathedral, an
exercise in the Gothic Revival
completed in 1888, stands in
splendour on Fifth Avenue
and provides an oasis for visitors from the hurry of the
avenue outside. But it isn't the
first St Patrick's in the city – to
find that one you need to go
to Little Italy on the Lower
East Side and search out St
Patrick's at 264 Mulberry
Street. Here, damaged by fire
in 1866, rather forlorn and
needing a facelift, is the
Gothic Revival original of
1815, seat of the first Catholic
Archbishop of New York.

May. The most famous is **San Gennaro's** in Little Italy, where you can nosh on Italian food as you parade under festive lights; and newly established Indian settlements (there are several 'Little Indias') offer Hindu celebrations such as **Diwali**. This is a major Hindu religious festival honouring the goddess of Wealth. It is characterized by feasting, presents and the lighting of lamps.

Many of these events are ethnic, yet wherever you come from, you will feel welcome. For dates and information on such events the Convention and Visitors' Bureau has listings (*see* p. 121).

The Arts

New York as a place just to eat, shop and indulge yourself wouldn't bring in many tourists, and with no arts the city would be a poor place. This is one of the liveliest and most creative places on the planet. Without **Broadway**, without magnificent museums, libraries and galleries, without book and record shops, without buzzing and intriguing centres of painting, sculpture and writing, without that incredible parade of architecture, there would indeed be very few reasons to come here. It's all going on non-stop in such vital centres as Midtown, Greenwich Village, SoHo, TriBeCa and the Upper West Side, with the added attraction of their parades of unusual characters.

Right: *The Metropolitan Museum of Art. Spacious art galleries, both public and private, make NYC a leader in the art world.*

Theatre

To find out what's on in Broadway, check newspapers and weekly arts guides. There are always the big musical and dramatic play hits, and these can be expensive, but there is a range of ticket prices and some bargains. The top talent performs on Broadway, from box office stars to supporting actors, dancers and singers, directors and designers. Performances usually start on Tuesday and carry on to Sunday. Be sure to book.

Above: *Radio City Music Hall is a big attraction, and a monument to the Art Deco style.*

The same goes for the lively movement known as Off-Broadway, which has a range of theatres all over Midtown and in the East and West Village. Often these smaller houses will have unusual, provocative plays with top artists and some, such as the lively **Manhattan Project**, often bring new shows to Broadway and beyond.

Literary New York

New York has always been a hive for writers, from the great names of the last century (**Henry James**, **Edith Wharton and Willa Cather**) to more recent literary luminaries. Many spent time away in Europe, but unfailingly drew on New York for experience and background. A number of hotels are famous for their associations: the **Algonquin** drew the wits of the 1920s and the **Chelsea Hotel** is currently a meeting place for playwrights and poets.

Many writers chose Greenwich Village as their preferred place and you will come across plaques on the various houses in which they lived. Today it's more likely that working writers will live on the Upper West Side, a place of old apartment buildings. It's a feisty area with a life of its own. There are also lots of bookshops and food emporiums along Upper Broadway.

CHEAP SEATS

On **Times Square** is an unusual and very popular booth where people queue every day for low-price tickets to shows. Called simply **TKTS**, it offers a range of shows for both off- and on-Broadway matinees and evening performances, day of the performance only, usually at half-price plus a small fee. The daily allocation of seats can be small, so some do sell out. Shows offered are indicated on notice boards, and can include some of the big hits. At half-price you can afford to be adventurous, so check for unusual offers.

Above: *Carnegie Hall hosts all kinds of concerts. Luckily, efforts to pull it down were thwarted.*
Opposite above: *Bargains on- and off-Broadway at TKTS Booth on Times Square. Day of performance sales only.*

DON'T FORGET YOUR GLASSES

The average theatre here is large, so for seats far from the stage, you will need opera glasses. This applies to the **Met** in particular. Smart and very New York, its huge foyers are decorated with paintings and a mass of flowers on a gala night. At the **New York State Theater** there are fine large foyers with huge sculptures of standing females. You may walk around during interval, and on warm evenings, people often spill out on to the balconies or the plaza.

Music and Dance

New York is a music town and you can find much of it here, from symphony concerts to recitals, band events and pop concerts. In summer the parks often have open-air concerts which are free and very popular. **Carnegie Hall** is world renowned, and at **Lincoln Center** there are packed programmes. Don't neglect the nearby **Juilliard School** for small events of new music.

For major pop concerts, venues like **Madison Square Garden**, **Shea Stadium** and **Meadowlands**, or the prestigious **Avery Fisher Hall** cater for the crowds. For major black stars (and minor on Wednesday Amateur Night), the new-look **Apollo Theater** on West 125th Street is back in business. It features top entertainers performing the blues, gospel and jazz. Other live music venues include **The Beacon** on West 74th Street and **The Ritz** on West 54th Street. Check the freesheets or the *New York Times*, for current concert schedules.

The New York City Ballet is resident dance company at the State Theater. Just like the Met, it is used by visiting companies when the principal occupant is touring or on leave. This company continues in the style of George Balanchine, who founded it and an evening here can be very exciting.

As dance is such a big interest in New York there is much activity, from classical to modern and experimental. See alternative publications or the *Village Voice*.

Opera

The **Lincoln Center** is synonymous with opera and dance. One of the few companies to pursue an expensive repertory system is the **Metropolitan Opera**, with a different work on every night except Sundays. There are also ballet events when the opera season is not in progress.

Architecture

It is hard to find much in New York that pre-dates the mid-19th century. In the East Village and Chelsea, in Lower Manhattan, you'll discover a few early and often isolated examples of **Federal** architecture from redbrick residences to the first brownstones. You will also find some later, interesting architectural styles, notably the marvellous cast-iron fronted warehouse buildings of SoHo. There was a flowering of exotic factory and office buildings 150 years ago and there are examples along lower Broadway and a few in the Financial District. In addition, there are some splendid examples of the **Art Deco** period that flourished during the opulent 1920s. These exotically sculpted, sometimes gilded and tiled buildings can be found all over the city, but particularly in Midtown. If you only take in one example of the style, go to the **Rockefeller Center** and **Radio City Music Hall**, or eat at the **Waldorf-Astoria** or the stunning restaurant at the **Essex House Hotel**.

New York shines in modern buildings too, mostly imperious glass and steel shafts noted for their pure simplicity. A recent exotic addition is the **Four Seasons Hotel**, which rises like a stern Egyptian temple on 57th Street, its corners knobbed with light fixtures like perched vultures, yet containing utter luxury within.

Below: *Art Deco is everywhere. Look for small elegant details too, both inside and out.*

Above: *Baseball is America's summer sport and popular with kids.*
Opposite: *Food on road-side stands looks and smells good. But choose carefully.*

Sport and Recreation

New York is a major centre for all sports, though the popular ones such as baseball (April–October) and American Football (August–December) are outstanding. **The Mets** (the local baseball team) meet at Shea Stadium (Roosevelt Avenue in Flushing), the **New York Yankees** at River Stadium in the Bronx. Football is played at the Giants' Stadium in Rutherford, New Jersey and the teams are the **Giants** and the **Jets**. Note that tickets for these events are very hard to come by.

Basketball, also very popular, (November–April) has one main team, the **Knickerbockers**, or 'Knicks', at Madison Square Garden. Ice Hockey teams (October–April) are the **New York Rangers** and the **New Jersey Devils**, the former at Madison Square Garden.

Other sports are available to the visitor in bewildering array. You can go bowling or boating, running or roller-blading, swimming or skating. You can play golf, squash or tennis, and there are fitness classes on offer all over town. There's horse riding in Central Park and in Brooklyn, as well as several race tracks. Riding and exercise trails in Brooklyn and the suburbs can be found in the city's parks and beaches.

Food and Drink

New York is one of those great gastronomic centres where the food range is enormous. It has some of the best food in the world and there are many very good restaurants, mainly in Midtown, Chinatown and the Village. New York is a city of many styles and a place where **French food** really *is* French and not an imitation, as so often happens. Many French restaurateurs have moved to the city, particularly **Bretons**, and have opened upper-crust establishments, often luring leading French chefs to join their team.

There are also small and comfortable eateries where you can obtain a set-price meal that might make you feel you were in a lively French provincial city, if it weren't for the roar of the New York traffic just beyond the door.

Other than French and hearty native New York food (and there's nothing better, from the fresh seafood of Long Island to luscious Caesar salads, or steaks from the Mid-West), there's a mouth-watering selection of different foods that you could sample for months and still not have gone through the whole menu. Add to these many small neighbourhood diners where a good breakfast can be very cheap – and a waitress will refill your cup at no extra charge. Children will love these straightforward American places which are popular with the locals and Americans visiting out-of-town. You can either sit at the counter or at tables and eat well-filled sandwiches or truly fat and mouth-watering hamburgers.

If you are on a budget, eating can be very cheap if you live on hot dogs or salads. Food and drink, particularly for light eating, has improved in the stations. Try the famous (but expensive) **Oyster Bar** at Grand Central. There are many food stalls and barrows in street corners, offering cheap snacks. For coffee and conversation, the new places are the bookshops, where you'll find refreshment areas among the shelves, and these new arrivals stay open till late.

There's good news if you plan to eat around the Broadway theatre and cabaret area. The Theater District in the **west 40s** is undergoing a revival. **Eighth Avenue** is being cleaned up with a section devoted to restaurants. Newly revamped hotels in the area are smartening up too: the **Paramount** and the **Millennium** offer a chance to eat right in the midst of things.

> ### EATING IN HOTELS
>
> You can eat extremely well in hotels in New York, many of them having renowned dining rooms and star chefs. **The Plaza** has patrician rooms and views of the park. Try the nearby **Essex House** for inventive dishes at their restaurant overlooking the park. There's delightful, intimate dining in a charming ground floor restaurant at the patrician **Mark Hotel** on East 77th Street, or go over the top and have a spectacular meal cooked by a top American chef at the **Four Seasons**, New York's most extraordinary hotel. Thank the gods of good food that all the eateries in this class take credit cards!

WINE

Although you can choose from a wide range of the world's best in New York, you may want to sample a few American wines. Many chefs will gladly introduce you to the 'local' wines, though NY State wines aren't for the connoisseur. The best wine comes from further afield, especially from the West Coast, where the Californian vineyards are long-established, but good bottles (particularly white) are emerging from Washington State.

Opposite: *NY bars are popular with locals and, besides drinks, bar food is usually good.*
Below: *There's one word for Chinatown: crowded. Even the restaurants have moved off the street and on to upper floors.*

If there's one place you shouldn't miss it's **Chinatown** where there are a vast number of Oriental styles and dishes. In this tight area, just north of the Financial District, there is every type of restaurant available, from the cheap to the flamboyant, all mixed in with shops, markets and bars. It is hard to go wrong here, and prices are usually not that expensive. If it's a snack, dinner, or day-long dim sum you are after, you'll find it here. The city's Chinatown may be small compared with San Francisco's, but it is a paradise for eaters, and highly recommended by local food critics too. Be warned: this is New York and writing about food and drink can be as arcane and folly ridden as some London or Paris reviews. Restaurants come and go quickly.

Next-door to Chinatown in **Little Italy** you can eat well, but bear in mind the food here is **Southern Italian**. Most immigrants came from Sicily and the south so it's solid pasta-and-heavy-tomato-sauce fare, and it's not cheap either. Look for seasonal celebrations in the city when food stalls are set up and you can try local snacks from Greek to Ukrainian or Cuban to Haitian, depending on the district. In New York the soul food (such as ribs, greens, corn bread, muffins and black-eyed beans) of the black community is worth trying too.

Drinks and Bars

Drinking in New York is a dream, whether your tipple is wine, beer, or those wondrous cocktails mixed with verve that really taste of liquor and give an instant heady glow. You can have straight drinks in your hotel bar, romantic cocktails in lofty settings overlooking Manhattan, or dip into neighbourhood bars where half the clientele will be watching a game on the ubiquitous TV. Irish bars abound, especially along Second and Third Avenues, and probably the most atmospheric one is McSorley's in the Village, a classic hangout where Woody Allen drinks and sometimes plays jazz.

Another good thing about New York is that whatever atmosphere you are looking for in a bar, you will find. Bars vary: from singles to sophisticated, arty to odd, theatrical caves or thumping musical dives, gregarious to gay. The selection is enormous and it is changing all the time. The opening hours can go on forever: often, closing-time merely means the doors shut in the early morning hours from 04:00–06:00 in order to clean up the joint. As a result many bars don't get going until very late at night, especially at weekends. If this is your scene you could be in heaven.

ETHNIC RESTAURANTS

It's not so long ago that it wasn't easy to find a good Indian restaurant in the city but the influx of Asians over the past two decades has changed all that. They have been matched by Cubans, Koreans, Vietnamese, Thais, Japanese, Haitians, Central Americans and Russians, all bringing their own cuisines and an accompanying nostalgia for the food of their country. You may need to seek your selection out (Russia, for example, is centred by the sea in an area now known as Little Odessa), but the choice of foods is amazing.

TABLE TALK

• **à la mode:** with ice cream.
• **bagel:** chewy bread roll often served with lox (smoked salmon) and cream cheese.
• **broiled:** grilled.
• **dim sum:** tiny steamed dumplings filled with meat, fish or vegetables.
• **eggs:** ask for them 'sunny side up' and they'll be fried on one side only; 'over easy', fried quickly on both sides.
• **egg cream:** delicious concoction of iced milk, chocolate syrup and soda water.
• **hash browns:** fried potatoes with onion.
• **hero:** French bread sandwich.
• **jerk:** hot barbecued pork or chicken.
• **knish:** savoury dough filled with cheese or potato.
• **pretzel:** savoury bread twist sold on street corners.
• **check:** bill.

2
Lower Manhattan

The tip of Manhattan Island is where New York City was born three centuries ago, but there's very little of that early past left. Of the first Dutch settlements nothing remains, and of the British Colonial era very little. As New York prospered in the 18th century many handsome residential buildings were built here; few survive, though the restored **Fraunces Tavern** on Pearl Street will give some idea of what the early city looked like.

Much of Lower Manhattan is infill from the time the Dutch started to break down hills, flatten out building areas, or to dig canals. They started a process which has never stopped, the most evident development of recent years being the huge **World Trade Center**. During the turbulent times of building, rebuilding, filling in land and building yet again, to arrive at the towers of the modern city of today, much has been swept away in the name of progress. In the eager haste to make money history has always slipped to a back place, and only comparatively recently has the city taken any pride in its exciting and fast-moving past.

What you see now is a business city, with few residents, receiving a huge influx of office workers every day. The **Financial District** stands firmly on old New York: with only tiny islands of the old, like St Paul's Chapel. As the Financial District ends, the sleek corporate skyscrapers are replaced by old warehouses and piers, now restored as the **South Street Seaport**. The Civic Center, a hive of government buildings and law courts lies nearby.

DON'T MISS

*** Statue of Liberty: New York's symbol of freedom.
*** Staten Island Ferry: for the best views in NY.
** South Street Seaport: a lively museum.
** Battery Park: has a superb waterfront view.
* Ellis Island: retells the story of American immigrants.
* World Trade Center: two of the tallest buildings in the world.

Opposite: *A glorious gift to the USA from France in the 1880s, the Statue of Liberty is spectacular.*

THE BEST OF LOWER MANHATTAN

Without doubt, after Midtown, this is one of the most popular parts of Manhattan for visitors. Apart from exploring, it is also a magnificent sight, whether seen from a ferry, from Brooklyn Heights, or from a helicopter.

Battery Park **

At the foot of Manhattan Island is Battery Park, a green space of 21 acres (8.5ha) that's also a result of infill. There are marvellous harbour views. The park takes its name from the line-up of cannons once surmounting the nearby circular stone fort. Boats leave for the Statue of Liberty, Ellis Island and Staten Island from the park's docks.

Castle Clinton National Monument *

Like its twin **Fort Williams**, across the water at the East Battery, Castle Clinton was built in 1808 to protect the city. When peace and independence made the fortress redundant, it was roofed over and became a music hall. Among the stars of the day who performed, the 'Swedish nightingale', Jenny Lind sang for the first time in America here in 1850. In 1896 Castle Clinton became the **New York Aquarium** (now in Brooklyn) but today is a National Historic Monument with exhibits on the history of New York. Open 08:30–17:00 daily.

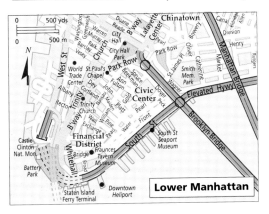

Lower Manhattan

Statue of Liberty ***

A gift from the French, Liberty, a magnificent work by French sculptor Frédéric Bartholdi, and now the symbol of New York, almost didn't make it. She nearly foundered at sea, and on arrival had to wait in huge chunks to be assembled, then for money to be raised by donations before being raised on her pedestal in 1886. The statue is 305ft (93m) high from ground to torch and offers fine views from its crown and observation deck. There's also a museum of immigration. Open 09:30–17:00 daily, but it's advisable to go early if you wish to climb up inside the statue (after an elevator ride) into the crown.

Ellis Island *

This is a national monument to the more than 17 million New Americans who arrived here between 1892 and 1954. A major refurbishment has provided this one-time entry point with attractions dealing with the island's adaptation and a complete history of the new arrivals. It touchingly retells the story of the great immigration which began in the mid-19th century; note the promenade beside a wall commemorating the names of 400,000 American immigrants. Open 09:30–17:00 daily.

Above: *Views of Manhattan from a high harbour point.*
Below: *The old Staten Island ferries, serving commuters, make a great free ride.*

Staten Island Ferry ***

It's a pity more people don't explore this option, for the Staten Island Ferry is free for foot passengers. You get a marvellous sightseeing voyage of the **Statue of Liberty** and **Ellis Island**, and when crossing the harbour, you see the maritime traffic crowding the water. Disembark from the ferry and explore the surprisingly large and tranquil Staten Island (*see* p. 105) and look back to the grand spectacle of Manhattan rising magnificently from the waves.

Museum of the American Indian *

Behind the ornate façade of the **United States Custom House** on Bowling Green lies this interesting museum, with one of the largest collections of material concerning Native Americans in the world. It forms part of the **Smithsonian Institution** and is a fascinating repository of artefacts from most of the hundreds of tribes that once inhabited the huge area we know now as the United States.

World Trade Center *

Its 110-storey twin towers, 1350ft (405m) high, dominate Manhattan's skyline. Take the elevator to the observation decks for unparalleled views of the city. The elevator takes 58 seconds to reach the 107th floor. Other modern developments nearby include **Battery Park City** and the **World Financial Center**. This has a dazzling, high glass atrium called the **Winter Garden** with shops and cafés – an exotic, palm-shaded place for a stroll or a drink and a place to appreciate the busy harbour, too.

OTHER MUSEUMS AND PLACES OF INTEREST

There are several other fascinating museums in this part of Manhattan. Look out for the **Museum of Jewish Heritage**, an oddly shaped building just north of Battery Park housing material concerning the Holocaust. In the Federal Hall National Memorial is the **Museum of American Constitutional Government.** A collection of modern art from the **Whitney Museum** (downtown branch) is in the foyer of 1 Federal Reserve Plaza. Outdated government buildings, banks and offices are being recycled as well.

FRAUNCES TAVERN

This handsome brick Georgian building, with its colonial air, is actually a fake. This is because it is a replica of the original tavern which was built in 1719. However, it still retains a sense of what it must have been like in 1783, when General Washington made a farewell speech to his officers here. There are spacious rooms with fireplaces; you can also eat and drink in 'Colonial style' here during the working week. Upstairs is a museum on the War of Independence.

Among the banks and businesses, note **One Wall Street** which has an impressive Art Deco banking hall, and the **Federal Reserve Bank**. Like the City of London, churches are really the only old buildings remaining. **Trinity Church**, right in the middle on Broadway at Wall Street, with its graveyard is one example (over 150 years old, it is the third church on the site). **St Paul's Chapel** is the oldest (built not long after its London model, St Martin-in-the-Fields, in 1766) and contains Washington's own private pew.

See also the **US Courthouse** with its gold pyramidal roof on Foley Square and the **New York Stock Exchange** at Broad Street. Here, visitors can watch the busy stock and bond traders from a gallery which overlooks the trading floor. Also noteworthy is the **Federal Hall National Monument**, a version of the Parthenon in the finest Greek Revival style. Although it wasn't built when he took the oath, a statue of **George Washington** before it marks the spot where he became president in 1789.

FILLING IN THE GAPS

Much of Lower Manhattan is infill from the time the Dutch started to break down hills, flatten out building areas, or dig canals. This has continued. The most evident development of recent years is the World Trade Center, standing like the two vast legs of a colossus, and whose sombre slabs can be seen for miles. Ascend to the top for wide-ranging views from an Observation Deck. Recycling the city resulted in the waterfront being pushed back from Pearl Street to Water Street, then Front Street. By 1820 it was South Street that eventually faced the East River.

THE VANISHED CITY

Much of this part of the city has vanished, including major skyscrapers such as the Singer Building, a domed tower in the Beaux-Arts style, the Tribune Building, and many small and often elegant warehouse and loft buildings. It's worth getting a picture book showing Lower Manhattan as it was 30 years ago. Since then whole streets have vanished so take a camera and record. Next time the view won't be the same!

Opposite: *The Financial Center's Winter Garden is a very popular place to eat.*
Left: *In Lower Manhattan modern glass and steel contrast with reproductions of classic styles.*

CORRUPTION IN THE CITY

In City Hall Park there is another building of considerable interest, which reflects a time when the city was run by a corrupt regime in the mid-19th century. Named after 'Boss' Tweed, the foundations of the **Tweed Courthouse** were sunk in 1862 and a great part of the many millions it cost were sunk too, without trace, into the political machine. There was so much anger at this filtering of public funds that the rule of blatant profiteering by Tweed's party was eventually terminated. Visit the courthouse to see its Victorian grandeur.

THE CIVIC CENTER AND SOUTH STREET SEAPORT

The **Civic Center** is an enclave of government buildings, a curiously mixed set, towards the north of the area. It is bordered by the **Financial District** and **Chinatown** (*see* pp. 44-45). Set in a green and paved open space, the curiously small **City Hall** is to be found here. Its staff and offices overspill into the nearby **Municipal Building**, with its fanciful roof decorations. As this is very much a business area, it can be all but empty on weekends.

City Hall *

The City Hall is a satisfyingly grand building, its style described as Baroque and Renaissance with Federal touches. There are lots of fanciful flourishes on this building! Completed in 1811, it is still the centre of New York City's government. Unfortunately one is no longer allowed inside to see its many treasures. City Hall used to be sheathed with marble on three sides, but not on the north side: at the time of its construction nobody could foresee how the city would spread beyond it. After the 1956 restoration, it was completely refaced in limestone. The surrounding space is **City Hall Park**, once the village green of the growing city.

South Street Seaport **

An evocative sight, not to be missed, is the South Street Seaport. Allow a lot of time to see this large place which has many aspects. A long-term project to mark the city's vital maritime history (it was founded because of the fine harbour), this 11-square block project well commemorates a time when New York was sovereign of the sea. Goods arrived from around the world and from the birth of the new country, trade increased with a fierce vitality. New York is still the nation's premier port.

In its great days South Street was a forest of masts and tackle, an image this very good 'living' museum attempts to perpetuate. Aside from visiting the seven sailing ships moored here, all meticulously restored, you can actually sail on one, the *Pioneer*, a schooner dating from 1885, or take harbour cruises on the replicas of old craft often in the evening for music and drinks. **Seaport Liberty Cruise** ships go from Pier 16 and offer a 60-minute narrated trip. Jazz concerts are held at the Seaport in the warm summer months.

Above: *The famed Brooklyn Bridge holds an affectionate place in the minds of New Yorkers.*

Opposite: *South Street Seaport isn't just a museum, there are lots of shops as well.*

The Old Docks **

Around South Street was a seething waterside dock area which has totally vanished. You can recapture some of the feeling of those lively, dangerous days in the nearby restored 19th-century buildings containing maritime exhibitions, an archaeological presentation at 17 State Street called **New York Unearthed**, and a 19th-century print shop and a children's centre. In the early 19th-century **Schermerhorn Row** are modern shops on the ground floor, as well as ships' chandlers and examples of sea-life providers.

This old chunk of Manhattan is renovated to appear as it once was: even with smart new shops and cafés, it gives a sense of an old dockside facility still. See also the **Battery Maritime Building** on South Street, a surviving example of a ferry dock from before the opening of the **Brooklyn Bridge** when scores of boats carried people back and forth across to Brooklyn. There is also the **Fulton Fish Market** which still sells fish, with guided tours if you want to see it in operation (check for opening times).

BROOKLYN BRIDGE

A handsome arch over the East River, and a New York legend, the Brooklyn Bridge was a 19th-century marvel. It went through many changes and there were many fatalities, including its creator, John Augustus Roebling. It opened in 1883 and took 14 years to build. The total span is almost 1600ft (488m) and it's a major artery feeding into Lower Manhattan, carrying many New York commuters every day. It's also a grandstand for pedestrians to view the river craft and the skyline from elevated footways.

3
Lower East Side and East Village

This is where the first waves of immigrants were shifted as their numbers grew. Landlords saw the possibility of cheap housing sites on the marshes east of the Bowery (then an undeveloped and unhealthy area), which together with the East Village south of 14th Street, makes up the Lower East Side belt. Hundreds of thousands of new settlers were herded into the low-lying area bounded by Lower Manhattan around **Canal Street** with **East Houston Street** to the north and the Bowery to the west.

This unwelcoming site was their introduction to a new life, but most immigrants didn't despair. They worked hard, made enough money to get out and moved on. Like the huge transit camp it has always been, the area still has a mean and despairing air. Take care when visiting as some sections away from the major avenues are not very safe.

The **Chinese** are still here, and so are the **Italians**, with well-marked areas of their own. The **Irish** were the first to put down roots, followed by **German**, **Jewish**, **Polish** and **Greek** influxes. The area has always been a migratory area and most recently it has been the **Hispanics** who have moved in, and with them people from the **Caribbean** islands. Many moved on, but it is still home for many **Puerto Ricans**, **African-Americans** and the Chinese, whose presence is most marked in over-crowded Chinatown in the southwest. Chinatown is developing so rapidly that it has taken in parts of Little Italy and the Jewish Lower East Side.

DON'T MISS

*** Chinatown: rundown and decrepit but there's marvellous food here.
* Cooper Union: school and gallery in a handsome brownstone building.
* Little Italy: Italian atmosphere and solid southern food.
* Lafayette Street: here you'll find the Colonnade and the Public Theater.
* Orchard Street: the market is renowned; everything is cheap.

Opposite: *Chinatown is filled with restaurants and gaudy neon signs.*

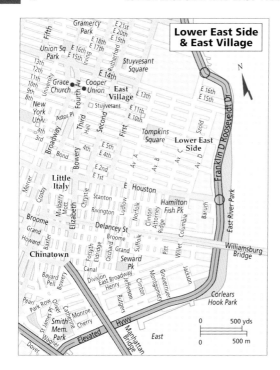

Lower East Side & East Village

LOWER EAST SIDE

A site for many festivals, from **Chinese New Year** to **San Gennaro**, the Lower East Side can for a time shed its unattractive image of packed old buildings and dilapidated shops and put on a show. But it is still an area of deprivation and poverty, so go by day and be prepared for a walk on the sad side.

The area is still the first stop for new immigrants, and it used to be a predominantly Jewish area. They were crammed into the newly erected apartment buildings, and the area had plenty of synagogues. At one time it was the largest Jewish settlement in the world as arrivals flooded in from the pogroms of Russia, dispossession in Hungary and Romania and, most recently, after persecution in Nazi Germany in the 1930s. The Lower East Side is now home to closely integrated settlements of Asians and Ukrainians.

Cashing in on the need for homes, from the middle of the 19th century developers rapidly constructed buildings that still line the streets today. Glad to find any roof, the new arrivals were crammed in. Many buildings had no running water and families had to share small apartments. In this lively, overcrowded area money was scarce, so it's not surprising that, aside from being a cheap place to live, bargain shopping has developed. On **Canal Street**, **Houston** and **14th Streets** especially there are many cheap shops, often overflowing on to the sidewalks.

A, B, C, D ...

Alphabet City on the eastern edge of this area is even more desolate in parts. This section, where avenues are lettered, was a drug centre and remains largely run down, with battered and sometimes ruined blocks spreading between Avenues A to D. Residents here try hard to rehabilitate and inject a feeling of community. There's a sculpture garden, and lively poetry readings are held at the Nuyorican Poets Café.

Left: *Street markets selling all kinds of goods can be found everywhere. Orchard Street is very popular.*
Below: *Most New Yorkers live on top of each other, in apartments. Alphabet City is particularly crowded and insalubrious.*

Orchard Street *

The place most people head for is Orchard Street, between Delancy Street and East Houston Street. If you don't mind the crowds, and the harried salespeople then you'll enjoy it. Orchard Street is the ultimate New York place for discount shopping for just about everything, but particularly clothes and fabrics, household goods and hardware. It's very busy on Sundays, as it was originally a market set up by Jewish merchants who didn't work on the Sabbath. It was deserted on Saturdays. Now newly-arrived Asian stallholders are trying to revive it.

Lower East Side Tenement Museum *

First built in 1856 on Orchard Street as the immigrant wave grew, this apartment building was one of many first homes for New Americans and is now listed as a National Historic Landmark. Within, you will find apartments of the era, some left exactly as they were when landlords turned the key on departing residents a century ago. The museum is part of a local walking tour and is open from 11:00–16:00 Tuesday–Friday; 10:00 –16:00 Saturday and Sunday.

The Bowery

People drive fast along the wide thoroughfare that is the
Bowery, where stops at traffic lights can mean boozy old
men trying to clean windshields with filthy rags. Not as
bad as it was, but a sad and desperate place, last home
for the derelicts and the dropouts of New York. They
spend the time panhandling the streets, sleeping rough,
and in the stark cold of winter huddled figures cluster
over pavement gratings emitting a little warmth.

Although its name has a romantic origin (from
the Dutch *bouwerie*, or a country lane, which it was
until New York's surge north) this main street of the
Lower East Side, along with First and Second avenues,
can be grim. Yet it remains a place some tourists want
to see. Its appeal must lie solely in seeing the dregs of
an opulent city. True, the spread of theatre activity in
New York has brought small playhouses and cafés
to unlikely places, and you will find a smattering of
theatre, dance and performance art here. There are
also cut-price stores and renovated loft apartments. In
general, however, the Bowery is a dreadful indictment
of our uncaring society.

There are some interesting buildings in the neighbourhood and both main avenues and side streets
reveal impressive commercial buildings, some of them
cast-iron and others with decorative brickwork. Look
for the **Bayard Building** (Bleecker at Crosby Street)
and, a bit further south, the home of a one-time humour
magazine, the **Puck Building**. This has droll sculptures
of the famous imp, top-hatted and mirror in hand, on
the corner and over the door of numbers 295–309
Lafayette Street.

Little Italy *

Once Canal Street was the border between Chinatown
and Little Italy, but this area is shrinking as the old folk
fade away and younger Italo-Americans are more likely
to be in New Jersey than here. So Chinatown, the southern neighbour, is cutting across Canal Street as it
expands and encroaches.

Little Italy still has an air of Southern Italy (Naples and Sicily, predominantly, as most immigrants came from there) and lots of places to eat filling meals. **Mulberry Street** is its main street, where the stress is more on heavy Sicilian styles and quantity (often vast dishes of pasta and thick tomato

sauces) than quality. Try **Luna** at no. 112 which is cheap and popular enough to cause queues and **Angelo's** at no. 146 for solid southern dishes. Cafés offer Italian coffee and pastries.

Little Italy is a very good area to go shopping. The food stores have plenty of salamis, freshly made pastas, cheeses and other imported delicacies. The most exciting time to visit is during the **Festival of San Gennaro** on 19 September when floats fill the streets, stands offer filling foods and the place is all lit up.

Above: *Restaurants provide big pasta meals (often Sicilian) in Little Italy.*
Below: *Unlike its neighbours, Chinatown grows and burgeons.*

Chinatown ***

This is one of the most fascinating areas of New York. Chinatown, at the southern edge of the Lower East Side, is many things to many people and one thing is sure: you can eat very well indeed here. But this is New York and we're on the Lower East Side, so forget the large and well ordered Chinese communities in London, Vancouver or San Francisco. This one is, by comparison, a mess.

It's fearfully crowded, grimy with cracked neon lights and disintegrating brick façades. But what a place – it's both smelly and

Above: *Chinatown is a lively mix of eateries, shops and even places of worship, like this Mott Street temple.*

PLACES TO EAT

Ducks hang everywhere in Chinese restaurants and the food smells are intoxicating. Try **The Golden Dragon** or the well-known and dependable **Peking Duck House** on Mott Street. The **Great Shanghai Restaurant**, 27 Division Street, has duck too but specializes in seafood. Back on Mott Street there are many Cantonese places: try no. 20. For a dim sum lunch the famous and busy **Hee Seung Fung** (HSF) at 46 The Bowery is cheap and delicious. Look for places the Chinese eat in, and if you like wine you may need to bring your own.

---

sophisticated, and it is real. As many as 150,000 Chinese live and work between the confines of the Bowery and Broadway, and many more of their relations from all over the Metropolitan Area come 'back home' on weekends. It was originally a defined area but now threatens to overspill on all sides.

The heart of the community is **Mott Street**, a restaurant alley with all sorts of eateries. Although the area is mainly Cantonese you can find excellent Shanghai, Pekingese and Szechwan style food. You can also eat from stalls and fill up on intriguing snacks. Eating can be a real bargain here, with plenty of choice and lots of special menus displayed to lure you in.

It's a pity not to indulge in Chinese foods and if you're not sure what to order, there are many dim sum restaurants. These give you a chance to sample tiny servings, often hot, often spicy, of a beguiling range of sometimes mysterious specialities. You are charged by the dish, usually piled up in little baskets. Dim sum houses serve from morning to mid-afternoon. Other places go from cheap to charming, decorated with florid, gilded dragons, fans, flowers, lanterns and figurines. Go at night when their multi-coloured neon signs compete with each other.

Shops selling all the usual Oriental merchandise, from scrolls and silk shoes and saucepans to kites and cricket cages and chopsticks, are sandwiched in these narrow streets. Upstairs rooms are often clubrooms. There's a temple with gilt buddhas on **Mott Street**, as well as the Chinatown Fair which is an amusement arcade. For those with a taste for the bizarre, the fair has a famous curiosity: its dancing and game-playing live chickens. Chinatown is a place with a life all of its own, and even the telephone booths are capped with painted and gilded pagodas.

East Village

Though well-known to New Yorkers, for visitors this is an amorphous area. The East Village is basically an extension of the Lower East Side, lying to the north, east from Fourth Avenue. Broadway and the Bowery are the two main north–south avenues.

More seedy, more raffish and much less charming or affluent than Greenwich Village itself, the East Village has served as a place where the less famous artist can live and still be near his or her preferred locality. So there are good reasons for a visit, though New Yorkers may try to put you off. It's safe enough in this part, but even so it's unwise to stray into too empty cross streets in the Lower East Side, especially after dark. This is basically a poor working quarter. Take care and stay on the well-lit main avenues. It's a place for new music, bizarre fashions and unusual gear. On some of the avenues are outrageous clothes and unusual antique and record shops which are often open late into the night.

The area abounds in historical connections. **St Mark's in the Bowery** on East 10th Street stands on the site of the chapel used by Peter Stuyvesant. **Cooper Union** is the birthplace of the NAACP (National Association for the Advancement of Coloured Peoples) and the American Red Cross. On Second Avenue above Houston

---

CHINATOWN MUSEUM

If you want to know more about the Chinese – see the displays of Sino-American history; photographs of Chinese life in the USA, or take a walking tour of the area, then go to the **Museum of Chinese in the Americas** on Mulberry and Bayard. This is an interesting centre for serious study of the phenomenon of Chinatown. There is a library that can be used and a bookshop.

WINING AND DINING

There's lots of choice for eating and drinking in the East Village, and many unusual places to choose from. It's noted for old-style bars such as **McSorley's Old Ale House** on East 7th Street, which claims to be the oldest in the country. Ethnic food abounds. There's still an **Italian** presence, with pastry shops north of 10th Street, and **Polish** restaurants. The strong **Ukrainian** flavour is reinforced by the restaurants as well as the annual festival which is held in May along East 7th Street, around the Ukrainian Church of St George. On East Sixth Street is another enclave of Indian settlers with many enticing restaurants.

Left: *Street life is a vital aspect of the East Village – you'll notice lots of graffiti spraypainted on the walls.*

THE COLONNADE

Originally a terrace of 13 stately town residences on Lafayette Place, this Greek Revival (1820s) row with its soaring pillars shows how grand the area once was. It has been cut in half and now only a section remains. Though sadly shabby and neglected, the area is looking up and the Colonnade still retains a patrician air.

Opposite above: *Originally Jewish, the bagel can be a snack meal.* **Opposite below:** *Look out for the Greek Revival and cast-iron façades. This one is on Lafayette Street.* **Below:** *New York's free libraries contain great literary treasures beside books!*

are **Stars of David** in the pavement with the names of Jewish stage performers who once were seen in the vanished Yiddish-speaking theatres here. Later literary stars such as Jack Kerouac and Allen Ginsberg were residents, establishing the Beat Generation. Note the unusual motifs and the stone sculptures fashioned in ancient styles over the doors and windows of many otherwise very ordinary buildings.

Lafayette Place *

At Astor Place several roads lead off including the once-elegant Lafayette Place. Here you'll find **The Colonnade**, where many famous people, including the novelists Washington Irving and Charles Dickens, lodged. Also on the wide street, the handsome old Astor Library is now the **Public Theater**, home of the New York Shakespeare Festival. Here many new and unusual productions have been seen, some transferring to Broadway. *Hair* and *A Chorus Line* started here. A great New Yorker, the late Joseph Papp struggled to maintain this institution (he was also responsible for initiating free performances of Shakespeare plays in Central Park). Enter its impressive lobbies and find out what is playing.

Old Merchant's House *

This unusual Federal-style residence was saved from destruction at 29 East 4th Street. It's a solitary example of how many streets once were, and how affluent families lived during the 19th century. The house is over 160 years old and has been carefully renovated as a typical family home of the period. Open 13:00–16:00 Sunday–Thursday, but closed Friday–Saturday.

Cooper Union *

A striking brownstone building on **Cooper Square**, this classic New York institution was set up by philanthropist Peter Cooper, a self-educated man who started this free technical and arts college in 1859. It was also the first college for adult education and the first in the US to be racially integrated. There's a gallery for exhibitions of American history and design.

Grace Church *

This lovely church was founded at a time when the area was still a smart place to live. It is hard to credit now, but there are still elegant brick houses on the cross streets around this imposing church on Broadway and 10th Street. Built mainly to serve wealthy Episcopal parishioners, the ornate steeple is a local landmark. A later marble addition replaced a wooden one even though it was thought that it would be too heavy for the church. Begun in 1843 and built in Gothic Revival style, this church gained for its designer, James Renwick, the contract to build the new St Patrick's Roman Catholic cathedral. He was only 23 when he designed Grace Church yet it is considered to be his finest achievement. Always crowded, **St Mark's Place** (the name for 8th Street beyond Third Avenue) has dives playing new music, shops with a mix of low chic and second-hand clothes and punk gear. The place is alive far into the night. Here are trendy clubs and small restaurants of all sorts, mainly grungy and rundown. Along with the ubiquitous punk and rock, folk and jazz all pulse loudly from the Bowery to the broad arrow of First Avenue.

North of 6th Street is the famous **Tompkins Square Park** where riots occurred in 1991 when homeless people were evicted because they had taken over the area. It has since been cleaned up and renovated, and is now a popular gathering place. Though it's not wise to hang about, there are good small shops around it. Read the anti-drug graffiti and look at the murals. Also check for newly placed historic site plaques.

> **UNKNOWN BROADWAY**
>
> In the East Village, Broadway is not the Great White Way but a market place. Here shops of all sorts are close together and the many cheap goods attract a very mixed crowd. They come from all over especially on weekends in warm weather, to saunter, to buy, but more likely to browse among the bargains.

4
Greenwich Village, SoHo and TriBeCa

Get ready for some unusual experiences, visions and fantasies! No, it's not New York's version of tinseltown Hollywood, this is life among real artists. Although more realistic and perhaps not as pretty as the Puccini opera, versions of La Bohème are going on all over this city, but especially in some favoured areas. **Greenwich Village**, **SoHo** and **TriBeCa** are three neighbouring areas where artists, from painters and sculptors, to film-makers and performers live and work. Every day the tourist tide floods through, having heard that this is the place for unusual sights that you certainly won't see anywhere else in the United States. In this part of town you won't be on your own with just a guide book for company – certainly not on a weekend. Art is big in New York and the city is a vital part of the international art city circuit. These areas are where the work is actually done.

The art movement started in **Greenwich Village**. It began as a real village (hence its name) before the flow of development engulfed it. But when the village became too expensive, artists moved to **SoHo** (South of Houston) in the early 1970s. As always happens, artists were soon followed by the crowd that wants to live like them without the pain of being poor, so the next area of decrepit commercial buildings to be taken over was **TriBeCa** or Triangle Below Canal Street. Even this run-down place is becoming fashionable. TriBeCa not only has fabulous galleries but also has very good, trendy restaurants on offer. However, the fortunate artists who got there first are still very much around.

DON'T MISS

***Commercial architecture:** the restored cast-iron façades are a unique New York feature.
*** Washington Square:** by day this central space is all atmosphere.
** SoHo on Sunday:** mass visits to galleries and shops.
* Christopher Street:** a walk to the river is an eye-opener.
* Food in the Village:** from specialist shops to small restaurants.

Opposite: *For many New Yorkers Washington Square Arch is the symbol of the Village.*

CABARET TIME!

The Village saw the blossoming of some of the first small theatres away from Broadway. Off-Broadway is well represented. So is Off-Off-Broadway, with cheaper spaces in less wholesome parts. Some of these theatres present quite surprising shows, although it's difficult to shock the neighbours. But this is the place for lively cafés and cabaret entertainment, and you can find plenty of small stages with stand-up comics, musicians and singers trying out their act.

GREENWICH VILLAGE

'The Village', as it is known, goes from **Houston Street** in the south to **14th Street** in the north, and from the **Hudson River** to **Fifth Avenue**, although its atmosphere continues beyond Fourth Avenue into what locals call 'the East Village', which is less respectable, cheaper, and in some ways more natural (*see* p. 45).

The Village is one of the parts of New York where streets are off-kilter (west of Sixth Avenue), so it can be confusing. There's plenty to see and do, with many galleries, cafés, restaurants and bars to choose from. The Village is an easy-going area with a relaxed attitude. You can live the way you like and it won't bother anyone in the least. Although basically a smart residential area, Greenwich Village still has a focus on creativity, and it can still trot out a few rather hardy eccentrics.

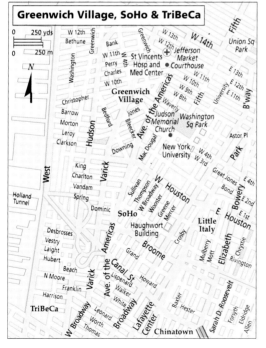

Artists are getting rarer in today's Village as prices of accommodation, particularly the space needed for big studios, have forced out the really creative people. Writers, needing less room, have clung on. The lovely old brownstones and brick 19th-century houses were homes to names such as Edgar Allan Poe and Henry James. Much harder to spot than painters or sculptors, today's writers still frequent the neighbourhood, and can be found in cafés, at lectures and even demonstrations. Poetry readings, literary events and book signings go on all over the place.

Left: *Neat 19th-century houses line the streets in red brick or brownstone.*
Below: *Murals have become a city art form, such as this DKNY grey one on Sixth Avenue.*

The Village is the place to find unusual books, clothes and foodstuffs, and there are often stalls set up on quiet sidestreets to sell unusual things such as carvings, candles and cult objects. If you like shopping, there are lots of opportunities to find unique items here. Wander up and down Eighth Street, the Avenue of the Americas (still known here as Sixth Avenue) and along such streets as **Christopher**, **Bleecker**, **Charles**, **Grove** and **Waverly Place** to get a feeling of this fascinating quarter.

Village Tour **

Head for Eighth Street to start. Greenwich Village is still full of that old creative urge even if it isn't old-style and impoverished any more. The architecture is rather eccentric but suits the bohemian air. The people can appear marvellously flamboyant. Crowds wander around after performances at the Cherry Lane, the Circle in the Square Downtown, the Lucille Lortel, or The Provincetown Playhouse on MacDougal Street. All this makes a parade that is fun to watch.

CENTRE POINT

The business and shopping hub of the Village is where Eighth Street runs into Sixth Avenue. Here a major subway stop (West Fourth Street station) unloads visitors and locals alike, and there are lots of news, flower and hotdog stands. The Village is excellent for good food shops: many small specialist ones and groceries spill out onto the sidewalks and liquor stores rub doorways with smart shops and galleries. Looming above busy Greenwich Avenue and 10th Street is the clock tower of the Jefferson Market Courthouse. In the evening the place is even livelier.

Below: *People chat, play chess and watch entertainers in Washington Square.*

Washington Square ★★★

Washington Square is set to one side of the Village, although it feels like the centre. This vibrant space is quintessential New York, whatever the season. Memories of great writers linger as kids play ball under the mature trees. The handsome stone arch which was completed in 1895 honours George Washington. The square also marks the beginning of Fifth Avenue and has been mentioned in literature. No. 16 is famed for being the setting for Henry James's novel *Washington Square*. Walk on the north side and you will catch glimpses of some fine façades. Some of them conceal apartments, such as no. 12, but no. 6 is a complete 1833 house.

Starting in the west you will find an area filled with students. They are the overflow from New York University (NYU) which extends for blocks around Washington Square. At the spacious **Astor Place** (with a notable subway station) there's a junk market and a modern sculpture of a big black cube. This is supposed to be movable so passers-by can interact and have a game with it. Here the liveliness of the area east of Washington Square is enhanced by various bookshops, some of them warrens, such as **The Strand** which is a vast, multi-million-volumed place at 12th Street and Broadway. There are many other shops, particularly along Fourth Avenue.

Note the **Judson Memorial Church** on the south side. This impressive Romanesque-style building is part of **New York University**, which clusters to the east of Washington Square. NYU students use the square as an impromptu campus, and figures hunch for what seems like an eternity over chess and board games. This is a good place to saunter and observe people.

There are many nice streets west of Fifth Avenue lined with handsome houses and good shops. Walk along Bleecker, Bedford and Christopher Street, and look for MacDougal Alley and Patchin Place for its charm. Don't miss the beautiful **Jefferson Market Courthouse**, with its ornate spires and turrets, on Greenwich Avenue at 10th Street. It was voted the fifth most beautiful building in America. 'Old Jeff' is now a library.

Above: *The Hudson River edges all of Manhattan and is often overlooked by tourists and, though run-down, is worthwhile.*

The Hudson River Side

The West Village starts at the Hudson, which used to be a dreary area of truck stops and sleazy low-life bars. It is improving, but this has always been a dockside place. Walk along West Street from the meat-packing area down to Canal Street for views to New Jersey and watch the cruise ships arrive.

There is an unusual example of civic planning, the **Bell Telephone Laboratories**, which became the artists' colony of **Westbeth**. This building was later redeveloped as apartments, yet without interior walls, so artists could have an open space or divide them as they wished.

The Gay Village ★★

It was here in 1969 that a confrontation between gay men and the New York police resulted in the **Stonewall Riots**, which are remembered as a milestone in the march towards gay liberation. The rioting incident led to the founding of the Gay Liberation Movement. In the Village haunts particularly they don't let you forget the fact that they've fought for and won their gay rights.

Most Village gay clubs, bars and shops are in the western sections, along and around **Christopher Street**. The street down to the river has always been a gay spot but recently this has faded a little. Now action is concentrated more in Uptown areas such as Columbus and Broadway, Third Avenue in the 50s, lower Eighth Avenue and Broadway up from Lincoln Center, but the Village life still makes for an eye-opening stroll.

INTERESTED IN PICTURES?

Many artists here are weekend amateurs trying to rub canvases with the real artists. To find professionals who really strive for their art is not easy, but it is possible. In upper rooms and studios in the three areas they are at work and some do show what they do: check noticeboards and even lampposts for announcements. Alternatively, pick up a copy of the *Village Voice* freesheet from a bar or café. This way you may ascend a creaky stair and mix with the knowing who are finding out what the talent has to offer. Try to get to the twice-yearly Washington Square exhibition which is held outdoors in June and September.

Right: In SoHo many old-fashioned businesses still exist, such as this corner bookshop.

SoHo ★★★

There was a time when SoHo (South of Houston) was declining because the industry which had created the district from the 19th century left it in empty desolation. But it was being eyed speculatively by a new crowd. Pushed out of Greenwich Village to the north by fast-rising rents in the 1960s, artists commandeered studio space here and squatted illegally, until eventually (and not untypically) New York recognized the place as a new art zone.

Inevitably the area became fashionable, and smart shops followed the lead of avant-garde galleries and bought up the space fronting the cobblestoned streets. The wondrously detailed cast-iron fronted buildings (once thought, falsely, to be fireproof) suddenly gained a new smart image and they were bought up, cleaned and scoured and their high, wide interior spaces opened up. Upper floors were rented out to the rich and trendy, and the ground floors were revamped and reborn as galleries and smart shops. New artists were turned away and only those lucky enough to have secured a space when the place was cheap, stayed on.

One of the first of these buildings was by James Bogardus and was put up in 1848 on Washington Street. SoHo is centred along West Broadway so branch from this thoroughfare and discover gems for yourself.

The style is particularly prevalent in the Broadway area between the Canal-and-Houston section, and one of the best known and most admired is the 1856 **Haughwort Building** which was made for a china and glass business.

The reason why so many cast-iron façades rose up at this time was because they could be quickly erected on constructions supported by inner beams and walls. Iron façades also allowed for the economical reproduction of detail so dear to the taste of the mid-19th century – elaborate moulding was far too costly to effect in stone. Most of these mouldings were made and cast by Badger's Architectural Iron Works.

The fact that many of these buildings are swathed and webbed with fire escapes shouldn't detract from the beauty of the buildings. Before these fire escapes were made mandatory, many people died in fires when trapped on their upper floors. Fortunately the unattractive changes that many of these buildings later received on their ground and first floors are slowly being altered. The high, airy interiors also lend themselves well to showing examples of modern art – particularly large canvases and monumental sculpture – and their height (often six to eight floors) means a good number of residents can be accommodated.

Above: *Sheets of glass, polished steel and modern art both indoors and out have changed SoHo.*
Below: *Small details on old buildings, often of a century ago, are fascinating to search out.*

CROSSING THE HUDSON

Oddly enough this isn't easy, though PATH operates under-river rail links. Take a bus across to **Weehawken** and walk along the riverside roads, or simply go out on the **Staten Island Ferry**, which keeps Jersey City on its right going out. The best way to see Manhattan is from the Jersey approach to the **Lincoln Tunnel**, which gives a spectacular view of the Island as you leave or arrive.

WHERE NEXT?

You'd think that artists were fed up with being pushed from one quarter to another, and would have all gone to New Jersey. Some have; after all, it's just across the Hudson. But the caravan is always ready to move on and new arrivals now look to other derelict areas. In the future it may be Brooklyn, Hoboken and Jersey City that are the new centres of art and creativity.

TriBeCa ★★

The selling off of SoHo to those with regular incomes able to pay much more for a slice of the area than the needy locals meant artists were on the move again. This time they migrated across the artery of **Canal Street** and southwest to the section they called **Triangle Below Canal Street**. Shortened to the convenient TriBeCa, it extends from this wide thoroughfare down to the edge of the **Financial District** and from the river to Broadway, and is New York's newest art colony.

Unlike SoHo, the area is only just experiencing development, and retains a hard, gritty and industrial edge. It is therefore more genuinely an artists' quarter. Despite the nearby presence of finance whiz-kids and a few stars such as Robert de Niro who are setting up film studios in its lofts, as well as a few shops and contemporary restaurants to please the foodies, the place is rundown – but chances are it won't be for long.

The cast-iron buildings of this part of the city are, like those of SoHo, worth a tour all to themselves. If your interest is architecture, these 150-year-old structures are monumental, reflecting many Classical styles, and often are very beautiful in themselves. You will find many examples here and in neighbouring

Below: *A jumble of buildings, hoardings, fire escapes and parking lots make up the local streetscapes of TriBeCa.*

SoHo, although many of this rich cache of cast-iron buildings are still unrestored. There's a movement by pressure groups to have the major streets made into landmark areas. Fine examples of cast-iron warehouse and commercial buildings can be found along **Broadway**, **White**, **Hudson**, **Duane** and **Harrison** streets. The streets are all named here, and the residents still frequent a few atmospheric old bars.

Visiting SoHo and TriBeCa Today
It's easy to wander these narrow canyon-like streets with guide book in hand, but why not sample the product? Watch out for notices of studio events and shows. Some are free while some charge a small fee for which you may get a glass of wine. You will see at first hand what the interiors of the buildings are like and how the real artists live and work.

Such open studio events are really for one thing – the artist wants to sell his or her work so perhaps you may find something you just can't live without. If art for you is merely dollars-on-the-wall and buying for future investment you'll be gambling so it is advisable to obtain inside information. A work of art, whatever the cost, is a souvenir of New York that nobody else will have!

Above: *A Harley Davidson in SoHo. All kinds of vehicles congregate on the streets of Lower Manhattan and motorbikes compete with the traffic.*

MOTHS TO THE FLAME

For many decades the city has been a powerful magnet for the arts. Every day dozens of young hopefuls from as far apart as Connecticut and California tumble off the bus or train, hoping to find fame and maybe money in Glitter City. For painter, writer, actor, singer, dancer or performance artist, New York offers the best possibilities of getting your act on. It'll be a hard path in such a tough city and just look at the competition – yet each arrival has stars in his or her eyes and the certainty that they are going to make it.

5
Chelsea and
Gramercy Park

North of 14th Street and below Midtown is largely residential. The old established neighbourhoods of **Chelsea** and **Gramercy Park** are small oases carefully protected in a larger spread and, although undramatic, these often surprisingly quiet streets offer a number of simple urban pleasures.

For those with an eye for fine architectural detail rather than whole buildings, there is a lot to take in – from ornate doorways to stone friezes and sculpted figures on façades. To wander through the streets of Chelsea, a planned community, is to see the real residential New York and maybe encounter New Yorkers, who are very proud of living in the neat old houses of these sophisticated areas.

Throughout this area the great avenues run straight north and south, with the exception of angled Broadway. Maroooned among a large amount of low-rise development are some surprising buildings. These are the early skyscrapers in the east 20s, not very tall in comparison with the nearby **Empire State Building** on 34th Street, but sensible, satisfying constructions with glinting gilding on roof and stonework. Among them is the newly cleaned **Flatiron Building**, one of the early skyscrapers to be built. It was originally called the **Fuller Building** but, owing to its unusual triangular shape, it became known as the Flatiron. Like so much of residential Manhattan, this is an intriguing mixture of buildings large and small, with much local interest if you are willing to take the time to search for it and see it.

DON'T MISS

*** Gramercy Park:
a reminder of how old
New York feels.
** Chelsea Hotel: a
venerable hostelry for
names in the arts.
** Madison Square: several
grand old skyscrapers are
grouped here.
* The Flatiron Building:
famed as one of the
first skyscrapers.
* Union Square: an open
space on busy 14th Street.

Opposite: *The distinctive Flatiron Building stands at the corner of Broadway and Fifth Avenue.*

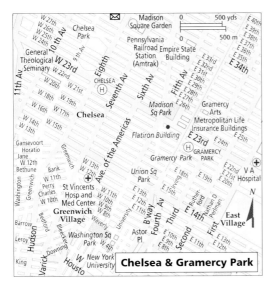

Chelsea & Gramercy Park

SIGHTS TO SEE

Before 1811 New York had little planning, adding streets as the town expanded. Then it was decided to impose a practical plan on northerly development, so 14th Street is important as it marks the beginning of the grid system which was established in that year.

From the main cross street of 14th Street, getting around the town is simple – there's none of the oddly-angled confusion of Lower Manhattan. All blocks are regular and all streets go directly north to south or east to west, with the exception of the old trail of Broadway and the thoroughfares running along the irregular edges of the island. The main avenues in the area are in general undistinguished; the important streets are 14th and 23rd, both wide two-lane thoroughfares with a variety of businesses, shops and plenty of life. For a walk, the eastern avenues (Lexington, Third and Second) offer more variety and interest, as they progress through contrasting neighbourhoods, while Broadway continuing from East 17th Street at the edge of Union Square has more interesting buildings and an uptown view.

Union Square *

This used to be a dreary, rundown space where even the decrepit New York pigeons were wary. But New York values its green places, and there aren't many. Although not quite recaptured from some of its unattractive inhabitants it has been redesigned with handsome pavilions, newly cleaned up and planted and it makes a welcome oasis and picnic place for workers. Its name comes from the union of Park Avenue South, Broadway and 14th Street, and it was once the centre for the Socialist Party's May Day celebrations.

The Early High Risers

It's hard to imagine New York without the skyscraper skyline as the city appeared in the 1920s. At that time the only tall buildings were clustered in this section – and they are still there, around the park known as Madison Square at 23rd Street.

Madison Square **

Just above Gramercy Park, where Madison Avenue begins, is a once undistinguished space at Broadway and 23rd. Before 1874 it was a cemetery and its 7 acres (2.8ha) are all that remain of a large area originally planned as a parade ground. Now a charming park, the trees make a soft frame for the classic old high risers and people often lunch here, enjoying the peace and quiet it has to offer.

Above: *Union Square was rundown, but is now more lively, with a Farmers' Market at weekends.*
Below: *Small green urban spaces, such as Madison Square, are much treasured in New York.*

The Flatiron Building *

Although 22 floors doesn't seem much to us today, it was a monster in 1902 when this dramatic building loomed over Fifth Avenue. It was then the biggest skyscraper New York had ever seen! Built to conform to a triangular plot at the angle of Broadway and Fifth, this grand old New York survivor is a prestigious office tower, and is now protected from the wreckers as it has been designated a City Landmark.

Below: *It's a marvellous clutter and unique, but don't expect the Chelsea to be a typical hotel!*

OLD RESIDENTIAL DISTRICTS

The two areas known as Chelsea and Gramercy Park are very attractive to New Yorkers and have some of the choicest and most valued properties beyond the pricey Upper East Side. These are areas not much visited by tourists, so if you want to get away from the herd, this is a good place to do it. There are no major sights, just a look at a New York that is old-style, refined and, as estate agents say, 'very desirable'.

Chelsea *

Chelsea was developed by Clement Moore who wrote the festive poem, *The Night Before Christmas*. Laid out in neat terraces of private houses, Chelsea was a model town of its time, stretching from 14th Street to 23rd and across to the Hudson. It is still known by the same name.

Much of the original work has gone, but one set of houses on 20th Street shows how the harmonious lay-out must have looked. This is **Cushman Row,** a row of fine brownstones, made more valuable because they face over an open space which is rare in Manhattan. It stands opposite the **Theological Seminary**, a large church with gardens. Walk a couple of blocks along Ninth Avenue and you reach the **London Terrace Apartments**. These are legendary in New York. At 22nd between Ninth and Tenth Avenues, they are known for the pomposity of the ceremonies invented to publicize these co-op apartments.

The Chelsea Hotel **

This large hotel fronting 23rd Street between Seventh and Eighth Avenues is a place that has received many illustrious art lovers. Look at the commemorative plaques on the outside – names that extend from acclaimed authors to pop groups. It remains popular for visiting literary stars.

Gramercy Park ★★

Although the actual place that this name applies to is a small East Side garden square at the foot of Lexington Avenue between 20th and 21st Streets, Gramercy Park's name resounds far beyond the 60 dwellings located on the square. It is a very smart address to have. The buildings edging the square were designed by some of the best-known architects.

People living around the actual garden have keys to it. A century and a half after it was created, Gramercy Park is now the only private garden of its kind in the city.

Above: *The quiet and ordered enclave around Gramercy Park is often tourist-free.*

Theodore Roosevelt's Birthplace ★

Just off Broadway on East 20th Street, the President's birthplace is hardly imposing, being one of a row of brownstone buildings of 1840. No. 28 has five rooms reflecting the style of the President's childhood. His family moved when he was 15 years old. Open 09:00– 17:00 Wednesday–Sunday.

The Players ★

A place to seek out here is the charming Players' Club, which is the city's principal club for theatre people. Special events (often for charity) are held here: it has a distinctive façade on east 20th Street. University and professional clubs are dotted around Midtown and several are notable. The Harvard Club at 27 West 44th has a floridly sculpted façade (the NYC Bar Association opposite is handsome Classical) and the Old Colony Club at 120 Madison was the first women's club in the city. The University Club at 1 West 54th adds ornament to Fifth Avenue. Because university and professional clubs have influential and wealthy members, these buildings resist development.

> **ARCHITECTURAL REMNANTS**
>
> For interesting local novelties, look for what's left of the one-time department store of **Siegel-Cooper** between 18th and 19th Streets. Sixth Avenue was the smart shopping street of Manhattan a century ago. Siegel-Cooper's neighbours of the time included Stern Brothers and B Altman's. The Classical Revival façade is typical of the period, pillared and decorated with flowers and foliage. For devotees of craftsmanship, Gramercy Park and streets off Fifth Avenue show fine details in casting, carving, wrought iron and stone.

6
Midtown

Midtown is divided into Upper and Lower Midtown, with the halfway mark being the main thorough-fare of 42nd Street from the Hudson to the East River. Upper Midtown goes up to 59th Street where Central Park begins, while Lower Midtown covers the diverse area between 23rd and 42nd streets.

Clustered around newly cleaned **Times Square** with its neon signs are the legendary showplaces of **Broadway** with enough theatre, cinema and allied attractions to keep you entertained for months! Great sights include many which are not to be missed: Park Avenue, the Empire State Building and the Chrysler Building, the Rockefeller Center, Grand Central Station, as well as the New York Public Library, the Chanin Building and the wonderful marble palazzo that is the Pierpont Morgan Library.

The one-time centre of Manhattan's shows, **42nd Street**, should be explored and its theatres and western part are now being renewed. Lower Midtown includes the Garment District in the west 30s and the many shops along West 34th Street. East is the district known as Murray Hill. **Fifth Avenue** and 34th Street are great shopping streets.

Midtown is the area most first-time visitors to the city will want to see initially, and maybe not leave at all, for most of Manhattan seems to be concentrated here in this middle belt of town. It certainly has some marvels on show and, one thing is certain, you won't be bored, though it would be a pity once you've tasted Midtown not to move out to explore other districts of the city.

DON'T MISS

*** Empire State Building: still a symbol of New York.
*** New York Public Library: a famous New York Institution.
*** Rockefeller Center: Art Deco glory.
** Chrysler Building: a monument to the car.
** Museum of Modern Art: a temple to the modernists.
** Times Square: simply the centre of town.
* Macy's: a shopper's heaven.

Opposite: *An elegant city landmark, the Empire State Building soars up and still dominates the skyline.*

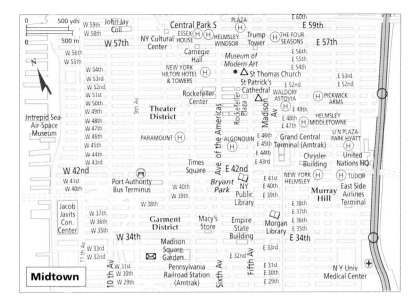

THE GARMENT DISTRICT *

New York is a fashion city, and that extends to the business of making clothes. It starts here, is promoted in glossy magazines, and what is designed and done here is news in the rest of the country. The west 30s around Seventh Avenue ('Fashion Avenue') are known as the Garment District and here in workrooms a great number of employees turn out ready-made clothes for shipment to points around the United States. Take a walk on any working day and you will see racks of clothes being swung out of workshops and warehouses into loading bays, bound for shops around the country. At 28th and Sixth Avenue is the Flower District. Visit early in the day.

Pennsylvania Station *

New York classics are always under threat, and one of the greats, the old Pennsylvania Station was a handsome Classical exercise in grand style, and partially inspired by the Baths of Caracalla in Rome. It was pulled down in 1966 and is a sad architectural loss. It is still there as the

Opposite: *You can't avoid seeing some of New York's famous buildings, and the Empire State often makes for a special photograph.*

city's main rail terminus, its Seventh Avenue entry marked by two stone eagles that once stood above its main entrance, but the station is now buried underground in the bowels of the **Madison Square Garden**. Even though this huge facility usefully hosts sports events, musical concerts and conventions, even circuses and commercial shows, and is a tourist draw, it is a sullen-looking edifice and architecturally sadly disappointing.

Across Eighth Avenue is the huge **Post Office** called the James A Farley Building. Its pillared grandeur once matched the vanished station. It, too, is scheduled for redevelopment – as an Amtrak railway station – but the developers have promised to keep the magnificent exterior untrammelled.

Empire State Building ***

This elegant building which still towers over 34th Street, contrasting with clusters of high buildings in Lower and Midtown, is a gem of Art Deco constructed during the Depression. Made famous as a landmark from the day it was completed, its steel frame enables it to stand tall at 1454ft (443m) high. It is often floodlit in colour and looks marvellous at sunset, sometimes with its head in the clouds, when light glints on windows and the metallic fittings on its spire, radio mast and beacon.

You can ascend the tower to the observation platforms. Note the lavish Art Deco lobbies and elevator banks. From the terrace on the 86th floor you gain great views and a trip up by express elevator is still one of the top Manhattan treats. Observatories open 09:30–24:00 daily.

MYTH AND LEGEND

The Empire State Building was destined for fame when it became the 'world's tallest' building, a title it held for several decades. It featured in the film *King Kong* where the ape appeared to be clutching the tower to his hairy chest while beating off aeroplanes that were attacking him. The Empire State is as famous as the Statue of Liberty as a symbol of the city.

VP PARKS

Throughout Midtown you'll find small urban spaces that have not been built on and which have been turned into small gardens – or **Vest Pocket Parks**. These little oases, smartly designed, often with a café and maybe even a waterfall, can be found around Midtown and are sometimes the result of trade-offs over 'air rights' by local high-rise buildings. They make a welcome place to sit and relax in especially on really hot days.

Below: *You can't miss Macy's – if shopping is your pleasure, you'll have fun here.*

SHOPPING ALONG WEST 34TH STREET

There are plenty of places to shop in this city from smart **Bloomingdale's** on upper Third Avenue to the popular Fifth Avenue stores, but the street many locals head for is still the favoured West 34th Street. This wide thoroughfare from Herald Square at Broadway to Eighth Avenue, is a hive of life with many shops and snack bars, its wide pavements crowded with shoppers seven days a week. One enormous store not to be missed is situated right at Broadway – **Macy's**.

Macy's *

New York just wouldn't be New York without Macy's. In this gigantic block-long, nine floor-and-basement department store you do have everything. It claims to be the largest department store in the world and even publishes its own directory. It used to have famous price wars with the long-departed Gimbel's, but now, the 140-year-old Macy's rules. If you aren't 'just looking' and can't find what you're after then consult the Visitor's Center which is situated on the mezzanine floor for information. You can also make bookings for restaurants and shows here. Macy's even provides a professional shoppers' service as well as an interpretation service.

Mid-West Side *

At the other end of 34th Street on 11th Avenue is the vast **Jacob K. Javits Conference Center**, named after a New York senator and one of the reasons why the city is a big player in the conference and meeting business. On Eighth Avenue between 40th and 42nd is the **Port Authority Bus Terminal**, a large modern multi-level building where thousands of commuters come in every day. It also handles long-

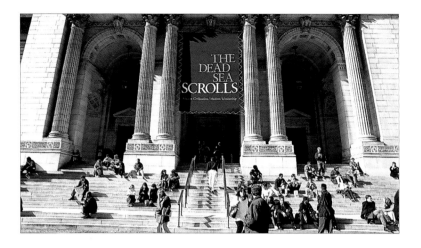

distance travel and since coach fares are cheap, it's very popular. It used to be an unpleasant place with a population of depressing down-and-outs but that has changed and it's now much more attractive with restaurants and coffee bars. The area behind it, from Ninth Avenue westwards, can be unsafe after dark.

Above: *The New York Public Library is a revered monument at 42nd and Fifth Avenue.*

New York Public Library ★★★

At one of the city's busiest intersections stands a grande dame of a building, the handsome Public Library. A popular meeting place is the flight of steps up to its impressive entry. It has a vast repository of documents, art, letters and books and there are frequent special exhibitions. The New York Public Library is a reference, and not a lending library (there are 80 branches around the city for that) but you are welcome to visit.

Built in stone in grandiose Beaux-Arts style the Library is as opulent within as without and has a vast entry hall. You ascend the baronial marble staircase to the vast Reading Room on the third floor. Be sure to ask about a free tour and remember to look out for the fountains and the pair of lions guarding the steps outside. Open Monday–Saturday. Opening hours vary. Closed Sunday.

THE BIG PARADE

Every November a big event hits New York and the TV screens across the entire country. It's the renowned Macy's Thanksgiving Day Parade when the store sponsors a huge procession of decorated floats, specially shaped helium balloons, crowds of costumed extras including cartoon characters, dancing and drumming bands and in the last float who do you think? Jolly old Santa Claus with his reindeer of course, to remind us all that at heart it's still a commercial event.

Right: *The UN Building occupies a large East River site and with its terraces and gardens it is a popular attraction for many visitors.*
Opposite: *The 1930s live on. Hidden during construction, the crowning needle was produced on completion of the Chrysler building.*

MURRAY HILL AND EAST 42ND STREET

Murray Hill is a largely residential area in the high 30s around Lexington and it is a pleasing area to explore. Around **Murray Hill** are several attractions, from the shops and bars of Third and Second avenues to a parade of striking buildings, many of them along East 42nd Street, which is well worth the long stroll.

Pierpont Morgan Library **

This immaculate, small Renaissance-style mansion of white marble containing a fabulous family collection is on East 36th Street. The Library, once home to the Morgan banking family, was built in 1904. This small, yet exquisite, collection was first opened to the public early in 1924 by the son, J Pierpont Morgan Junior. It has some quite extraordinary treasures within. In sober settings and ornate decors taken from European palaces this hoard of rare manuscripts, original music scores, precious stones and books – including a very rare

Gutenberg Bible – is one of the most fascinating in the city. It also offers guided tours. Open 10:30–17:00, Tuesdays–Saturdays and Sunday afternoons.

United Nations Building **

Over on 1st Avenue and East 44th Street, by the East River rises a striking slab of glass and steel. It's the United Nations Building which is open every day and offers regular tours. This is the place to go and see how this organization functions. There are visits to the chambers where the General Assembly sits as well as visits to various other counsel chambers. Look out for the Leger paintings in the Assembly Hall and the Chagall windows in the foyer. For lunch the UN restaurant is formal, but it's worth eating there if only to see the river views. Outside, flags of member nations flutter and the gardens by the river make a memorable walk. You can obtain free tickets at the information desk for certain sessions.

Chrysler Building **

A slender and impressive monument to **Art Deco**, much loved by New Yorkers, this famous skyscraper at Lexington and 42nd is the Chrysler Building. It was con-structed as the New York headquarters and additionally as a praise-poem to the Chrysler motor car. It is 77 storeys high! This enduring monument to the motor car is appropriately adorned with all sorts of decorative elements from grilles and ornaments to hub caps, friezes of 1930s motor cars, and symbols of energy. These are particularly noticable at night when the sleek grey-blue Chrysler bursts into dazzling light. It's unique, yet a typical example of New York's wonder-ful sense of excess in high Art Deco. Go inside and see the lobbies and the interior fittings.

CARNEGIE HALL

A revered concert hall in a high Victorian style, Carnegie Hall on West 57th Street is a place many artists are proud to play in. It's over a century old yet its acoustics are rated as first class. Most nights have different attractions from soloists to small groups. After you may glimpse the stars at the nearby Russian Tea Room at 150 West 57th Street.

Grand Central Station **

There are more amazing buildings along the stretch of 42nd Street. Facing Park Avenue South and, effectively cutting the famous avenue in half, is the vast **Grand Central Station** with its façade of a magnificent array of statues around a big gilded clock. It's just as fanciful inside with throngs of commuters thrusting through high-ceilinged marble halls. One place you shouldn't miss is the **Oyster Bar** with its shell shape harking back to the grand days when Grand Central ran many more trains than it does today. Above the station is the giant **Pan Am Building**, which irritates many New Yorkers because it dwarfs the station and cuts off the Park Avenue view.

Further along on the South side of 42nd Street is the 1930 **Daily News Building** in black slabs (note the huge rotating globe inside) and the handsome steel-and-glass atrium of the **Ford Foundation**. This building has a garden caged in glass, 12 storeys high which visitors can explore – great if you want to come out of the rain! The **Chanin Building** at 122 East 42nd Street is another Art Deco building of style with a lobby beautifully decorated in gilt and with unusually designed, graceful chandeliers.

Other notable buildings in the area include several churches. At Madison and 35th Street stands the **Church of the Incarnation**. Within are sculptures and Tiffany glass. The **Marble Collegiate Church** at Fifth Avenue and 29th Street has roots dating back to the Dutch occupation, but it's better known as the first church in America to have had an electric organ. At Madison and 34th Street, the **Church of the Transfiguration** is the home of New York's theatre folk – engagingly small, 'the little church around the corner' has the look of a country chapel, a certain fairytale charm in the city.

Below: *The very grand concourse of Grand Central Station.*

Left: *Tiffany's is not only a landmark on Fifth Avenue; it featured in Truman Capote's novel,* Breakfast at Tiffany's.

ANTIQUES

You might not think New York would be a place to find antiques, but this city thrives on auction sales, and serves up many surprises. There are antique marts with lots of stands here, fine for bargain hunting and browsing on a cold or damp day. Try the **Place des Antiquaires** at 125 East 57th, or not far off on Second Avenue, the **Manhattan Antique Center.**

FIFTH AVENUE – WEST SIDE

Fifth Avenue offers many sights to the visitor. Its famous stores line the avenue in midtown. Be sure to take a stroll from 34th up to 59th Street. There are a parade of shops from **Lord and Taylor's** to **Saks** and from **Tiffany's** to toyshops. You certainly won't be bored especially when the avenue changes like a kaleidoscope! Famous shops mingle with boutiques, as well as cut-price carpet stores and art and jewellery shops.

Best of all it's always busy with people, especially at the weekends and at festival times. Strolling along this part of Fifth Avenue you will truly feel that you are in the throbbing heart of a great metropolis.

Fifth Avenue is the dividing line for Midtown and one of New York's great walks. A major cross street, 57th, makes a marvellous walk especially if you like to window-shop – the galleries and boutiques of East 57th and uptown Madison Avenue are famous and often fabulous. At 59th, where Midtown ends, you arrive at Central Park South. This wide cross street is the southern border of Central Park with grand hotels such as **The Plaza** and **The Essex House** and glamorous restaurants offering wonderful views of the greenery just across the road. You can do the ultimate tourist thing here and rent a horse and carriage for a trot through the town and park. The apartment blocks here are most sought after because they face the park.

TOY SHOPS

Don't even think of visiting a toy-palace like **FAO Schwarz** at 767 Fifth Avenue at Christmas time unless you like to inflict punishment on yourself. Not only is the place crammed, but there are queues or 'line-ups' out in the cold on 58th Street waiting to get in. Once in the place it is like a gigantic game, with salespeople dressed in costume and uniform demonstrating all the latest toys and fads. Take kids if you can, but just keep a hold on the credit cards if you don't want a big bill. This one's an expensive bazaar.

Times Square ★★

It's still crowded and lit up with advertising signs but
has nevertheless retained some kind of glamour. The
square is actually a triangle extending from 42nd Street
to 45th Street, the point at which Seventh Avenue crosses
Broadway. There are many restaurants, bars and shops,
and best of all the nearby theatres of Broadway which
are a big lure to many visitors. Look for the half-price
booth called TKTS at the top of the square for bargains.
There are tourist information booths and a handy official
one at the old Embassy Theater lobby on Broadway,
open every day. *The New York Times*, the daily paper
that gave the square its name, occupies a grim set of
buildings on West 43rd Street. For many, Times Square
is quite simply the centre of town.

Rockefeller Center ★★★

Between 47th and 52nd Streets off Fifth Avenue, this
centre is one of New York's great pieces of urban planning. It has a set of stylish 1930s buildings, gardens and
walks set in 29 acres (11.7ha) at the heart of Midtown,
opposite St Patrick's Cathedral. The whole complex can
take quite a long time to see but do at least walk down

Below: *Times Square isn't
a square, it's a confluence of
roads. Once dilapidated and
dangerous, it's been cleaned
up in recent decades.*

Left: *During the year there are always crowds at the Rockefeller Center, and in the winter there's skating.*

the main avenue with its glorious flowery gardens to the central sunken plaza – a great place for New York socializing! The plaza is an open-air restaurant in summer and in winter it becomes a skating rink under the looming statue of Prometheus. There are lots of stylish shops and do take note of the individual detailing of this rich monument to Art Deco in metalwork, tiles, glass and sculptured works.

At the rear of the Rockefeller Center, within the complex itself, is a mammoth theatre that is a New York institution: **Radio City Music Hall**. It was opened in December 1932 after having been lovingly restored. With almost 6000 seats, this is America's showplace, host to a range of attractions, especially when the big Christmas Spectacular has the legendary Rockettes high-kicking. At other times of the year it is host to a range of attractions. In style it is high Art Deco, with fabulous decors – even the men's toilet is in the period! If you can't find time to

---

HELL'S KITCHEN

Although its picturesque name conjures up a descent into an inferno, this area of the west 40s and 50s over towards the Hudson is much tamer now. Once a quarter of poor new settlers and warren-like tenements, it's been improved and a new set of residents have moved in. Like neighbouring Eighth Avenue, it has been cleaned up but prostitutes can be fairly blatant on the sidewalks. Also from here up to 57th are the major theatres and a new restaurant area west of Eighth Avenue in the upper 40s which has added a touch of class to the area.

Right: *Sixth Avenue (or Avenue of the Americas) at the grand marquee of Radio City Music Hall.*
Opposite: *The Museum of Modern Art, with a host of treasures, always has a stream of visitors.*

see a show then take a tour for a modest fee. They last an hour and give you a marvellous introduction to both front and backstage aspects of a great American theatre.

American Craft Museum ★★

Just across the road from the Museum of Modern Art, and often overlooked as a result, is the American Craft Museum. It was founded in 1956 by the American Craft Council, the building being specially designed for the purpose, and its permanent collection today contains thousands of craft artefacts – from teapots to chairs to baskets to rugs – on four storeys. Open 11:30–19:30, Tuesday–Sunday. Closed Mondays. The library next door has a distinguished collection of children's books.

Museum of Modern Art ★★

To some New York visitors this is one of the greatest shows in the city. The Museum of Modern Art (MOMA) is a severe building at 11 West 53rd Street. Within are many treasures. If contemporary art is your pleasure, you won't want to miss it. Here you will find the great American artists, as well as famous Chagall, Mondrian and Picasso paintings. The museum is constantly chang-

---

THEATRES

Broadway theatres are big and renowned, and the good news is that they are busy again and new ones are being added. The dilapidated ones along 42nd Street are being restored, along with the street itself. Among the latest are the New Amsterdam and the American Airlines, and others will follow. Although large, many Broadway theatres have very limited foyer space.

ing and has as its special preserve all modern arts from photography to film, paintings to prints, bibelots to books as well as sculpture and architecture.

Since it first opened in 1929, MOMA has been pleasing and shocking the crowds and they still flock in. You may have to reserve tickets straight away if the film you want to see is going to be on at one of its cinemas. The sculpture garden, with amusing pieces by Alexander Calder, Rodin and solid nudes by Maillol, is overlooked by the Cafeteria and the Members' Dining Room which is open to the public. The entrance fee includes film tickets. On Fridays at MOMA you can make a small donation instead of paying an entrance fee.

> **MUSEUMS**
>
> Most of the city's museums gained their treasures from private collections. The rich New Yorkers are often commemorated with the names of individual galleries or extensions to the buildings. However, aside from grand galleries, many small museums can easily go unremarked in the city. If you have a specialist interest ranging from dolls to railway memorabilia, chances are there is a collection for you.

Classic Skyscrapers

The 40-year-old Seagram Building is one of the great beauties of Park Avenue; it houses the smart Four Seasons restaurant. The brownstone Villard Houses were important city residences of a century ago: now they are incorporated with a brassy glass tower into the Palace Hotel on Madison Avenue at 50th Street. Nearby the 1924 Crown Building on 57th Street is faced on its upper levels with gold leaf. Other notable classic Art Deco buildings include the General Electric, recently done up and renewed at 570 Lexington; the French building, bronze reliefs at ground floor, elaborate tiling on its tower at 45th and Fifth and the Fuller Building at 57th and Madison. Some buildings have gone out of their way to establish an eccentric style, such as the Chippendale chest effect on West 56th Street. At the foot of Manhattan the most prominent skyscrapers of the city are the plain twin towers of the World Trade Center.

FIFTH AVENUE – EAST SIDE

There are so many interesting sights in Midtown its hard to get them all in without resorting to a boring list. Many are central and are situated along Fifth Avenue, from the **Trump Tower** to the **Rockefeller Center**, but others are a bit off the track and worth searching for. Walk along the narrow Madison Avenue for a parade of old buildings bristling with decoration, though some only explode into the exotic at their summits.

Trump Tower *

The **Trump Tower** on Fifth Avenue is a newcomer, a spectacular building with a corner of its glittering glass façade shaved off to allow a tumble of trees and vegetation to hang dramatically over the avenue. You can go in and explore its huge atrium and shops.

The Waldorf-Astoria *

The truly grand be-flagged Waldorf-Astoria Hotel on Park Avenue at 49th Street didn't start off at this address, though it is now a more fashionable address than its original one. Before the Empire State was built, two cousins, Astor and Waldorf, had turned one-time

Below: *Within the Waldorf-Astoria the public rooms are a gilded dream of Art Deco grandeur.*

Left: *Tall, pointed Gothic arches, magnificent rose windows and sculptured columns make St Patrick's interior impressive.*
Below: *St Pat's, as New Yorkers call this cathedral, viewed from the sculptures from the Rockefeller Center's mall.*

family homes then on the site, into two hotels. Moved uptown to make way for the new skyscraper, the cousins amalgamated the hotels which became the famous Waldorf-Astoria, a lush Art Deco palace that has hosted many of the greatest names of the 20th century.

St Patrick's Cathedral ★★★

A twin-spired 19th-century Gothic construction, St Patrick's Cathedral is the seat of the cardinal of New York and America's biggest Catholic cathedral which is situated at the centre point of Fifth Avenue. Every year the Cathedral is the the focus of the St Patrick's Day Parade. It's very much a centre of worship, its cool interior flickering with candles. Nearby is St Thomas' Anglican church. A former mosque, elaborate inside and out with mosaics, became the **City Center Theater** on West 55th Street 50 years ago.

7
Upper East Side

The Upper East Side is New York's class act; the place most New Yorkers would prefer as an address if they could afford it and if they could only find a decent spot to perch in. Some residents have been holed up here for decades, and aren't about to give up apartments that probably seemed expensive when they moved in and are now bargains. As you might expect, the neighbourhood is filled with handsome, usually clean streets, a range of pleasant places to eat, many small art galleries and the best and smartest shops.

The Upper East Side is an area that extends from East 59th Street up to the top of Central Park at 108th Street where Spanish Harlem takes over. Underneath the central mall from 42nd Street glide the railroad lines from Grand Central Station; they are very discreetly covered over under Park Avenue's grassy central divide until they emerge at 94th Street.

The Upper East Side is bordered by the **East River** to one side and the great swathe of greenery to the west where **Central Park** ploughs its green patch among the high risers. It's New York's finest open space, its southern edge stretching from Fifth Avenue to Central Park West. The park borders one of the city's smartest thoroughfares: **Upper Fifth Avenue**, overlooking the park with a series of imposing apartment buildings for the most part with grand entrances and uniformed doormen. The area also has a distinctive European air with German and Middle Europeans in the north, while the Koreans and Vietnamese have opened up shops in the area.

DON'T MISS

*** **Central Park:** New York's own green acreage, with a popular zoo.
*** **Metropolitan Museum of Art:** a truly spectacular art gallery.
** **Upper Madison Avenue:** New York's most exclusive stores – with prices to match.
** **The Whitney Museum:** modern masterpieces.
*** **The Frick Collection:** great treasures in a sombre, grand setting.

Opposite: *During the icy winters, skating in Central Park is popular.*

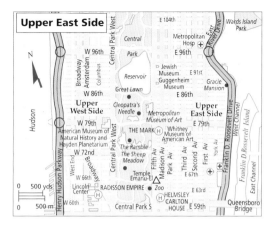

Upper East Side

N

Hudson

Henry Hudson Parkway

Broadway

West End

Amsterdam

Columbus

Central Park West

Central Park

E 104th

Wards Island Park

W 96th

Central Park

Metropolitan Hosp

E 96th

Reservoir

Jewish Museum

E 91st

Guggenheim Museum

Gracie Mansion

Great Lawn

W 86th

E 86th

Upper West Side

Cleopatra's Needle

Metropolitan Museum of Art

Upper East Side

E 79th

American Museum of Natural History and Hayden Planetarium

THE MARK (H)

Whitney Museum of American Art

W 72nd

The Ramble

The Sheep Meadow

Fifth Av

Madison Av

Park Av

Third Av

Second Av

First Av

York Av

Franklin D. Roosevelt Drive

West Channel

Roosevelt Island

East Channel

W 66th

Temple Emanu-El

E 67th

Broadway

0   500 yds

0   500 m

Lincoln Center (H)

RADISSON EMPIRE ● Zoo

E 63rd

W 60th

(H) HELMSLEY CARLTON HOUSE

Central Park S

E 59th

Queensboro Bridge

CENTRAL PARK ★★★

The park was first opted for purchase by the state as an open space in 1853 and a competition was launched for the design. It was won by Frederick Law Olmsted and Calvert Vaux, who converted nearly 850 acres (344ha) of wasteland into a wonderland. There are several lakes and ponds, and in the north is a reservoir circled by New York's foremost public running track. Although it is an urban park, with masses of statuary and such formal features as the **Bethesda Fountain** and terrace and the **Belvedere Castle**, there's lots of green space from the **Ramble** to the **Great Lawn** and **Sheep Meadow**. At the northern end is the formal **Conservatory Garden**. At 64th Street look for the newly revamped **Central Park Zoo**, which used to be free and rundown, but now they charge for its new look. There's a small collection of animals and a popular seal pool. Cars are banned at weekends.

Below: *Walking, jogging, cycling, skateboarding, or riding – the park attracts many activities.*

Very popular with plenty to do, in Central Park you can walk, jog, cycle or even ride; there's Shakespeare at the **Delacorte Theater** in summer and tennis on the courts near the reservoir. It's open all year round, but don't go at night, or wander around deserted places.

Upper Fifth Avenue **

The name Fifth Avenue is synonymous with smart New York and the wide cobbled sidewalk along the grand avenue reaches almost bucolic heights as it patrols Central Park. As you might expect, its name conjures up the image of the upper classes with their smart addresses. It's tree-shaded with its walks running by the low park wall, a fine place for a promenade or a place to take your expensive pooch.

The west side is smartest here, as a walk will soon show. A few of the old palatial houses that first claimed the turf a century ago still exist, and you almost expect to pay to breathe the air here, it's so exclusive.

Upper Madison Avenue **

Madison Avenue is narrower and more commercial, but paradise for those who like to window shop. The stores are often very expensive, specializing in particular things such as high fashion and interior decor items like antiques, Art Nouveau and Art Deco articles to Colonial furniture. The great auction houses can be visited, usually free, though you may need tickets to look at displays of coming auction items. Yet as this is New York there are still ordinary stores spliced in. Shopping is more straightforward along parallel **Lexington**, **Second** and **Third** avenues. Despite its name, **Park Avenue** is a dull boulevard with huge blocks of gloomy apartments.

Above: *Window displays on Fifth Avenue can be riveting, especially during Christmas when they vie for business with each other.*

BUILDINGS IN CENTRAL PARK

It's estimated that if all the constructions planned for Central Park by well-meaning (and some more commercially inclined) folk were built, the entire space between 59th Street and 110th would have been built over almost twice by now. Fortunately, there's a strong movement to keep the park green, but buildings that have elbowed in include the **Metropolitan Museum of Art**, the **Arsenal**, the **Zoo**, the **Delacorte Theater**, the **Tavern on the Green**, various stables, boat-houses and bandstands and a police station.

Right: *An old-style store with many departments, Bloomingdales is unique. It's expensive, but it is the place to find unusual gifts.*

Bloomingdale's *

Don't miss a visit to the favourite, expensive, and slightly eccentric store New Yorkers love at Lexington and 60th Street. '**Bloomies**' is the exotic showbiz store of New York and quite an institution. Fresh, trendy or fabulous, you'll find it here.

MUSEUMS

Ranged along Fifth Avenue is **Museum Mile**. This is the home of the **Museo del Barrio**; the **National Academy of Design**; the **Cooper–Hewitt/National Design Museum**, housed within a handsome mansion on 91st Street; the **Jewish Museum** at 92nd Street; the **Museum of the City of New York**; the **International Center of Photography**; the **Goethe–Institut** and others. Off First Avenue in Carl Schurz Park is the mayor's residence, Gracie Mansion, which can be visited (on Wednesdays by appointment).

Solomon R Guggenheim Museum *

The Guggenheim at 88th Street is a controversial building (some people dislike it) which was designed by Frank Lloyd Wright and is his only building in New York. It is shaped like a flower pot and consists of descending ramps loaded with abstract and impressionist paintings. Works you will see are by artists such as Picasso, Braque, Van Gogh and Chagall. Open 10:00–20:00 Friday–Wednesday.

The Metropolitan Museum of Art ***

This is simply one of the greatest repositories of art in the world. This palatial building on Fifth Avenue between 82nd and 86th streets should not be missed, whether you are fond of art or not. It's a showplace and a bit awe-inspiring; as you ascend the grand flight of steps you have a real sense of occasion.

Like the Louvre or the British Museum, this is a star collection of major items, and you can only hope to see a part of it in a day's visit. It's absolutely huge: its many rooms encompass not just a great number of pictures but also sculpture, decorative arts and furniture, arms and armour, costume, and a whole range of antiquities. In addition there are regular exhibitions, some of them major retrospectives of particular artists or movements.

> **STORAGE**
>
> A problem shared by all New Yorkers is where to put things. Museums have the same difficulty – multiplied several times. Not all works in big collections merit display, or are only available in private study areas. Reflect as you wander around the vast collection at the Met that nine-tenths of the Museum's holdings are reputedly in a storage tunnel under Fifth Avenue!

Below: *Frank Lloyd Wright liked to shock and his Guggenheim Museum is very controversial in its design.*

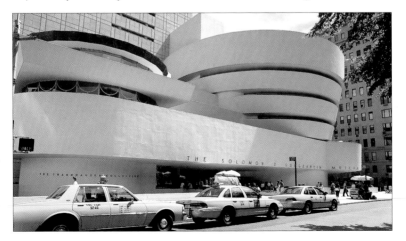

The American Wing is fabled, there are whole buildings from Ancient Egypt, an Assyrian lion, and rare and remarkable Vermeers. Van Gogh's *Irises* and *Cypresses* are here, too. Guided tours are available on request. There's a restaurant where you can snack or have a meal. Entry is by voluntary donations and you may give what you can afford, but it would be appreciated if you pay the full suggested amount, as this helps to cover the cost of special exhibitions, for which there is no additional charge or special ticketing. Open 09:30–17:15 Tuesday–Thursday, Sunday; 09:30– 20:45 Friday and Saturday.

The Frick Collection ***

This is a great star in the city's museum firmament and the kingly marble palace of a merchant baron is quite small – so it's possible to see it in a couple of hours. But it would be a pity not to linger before the marvellous paintings and lavish interior decors, with famous exhibits such as **Rembrandt's** *Polish Rider* and **Vermeer's** *Officer and the Laughing Girl* or **Gainsborough's** *Mall in St James's Park*, even if the building is rather rigid in style and feels a bit like a very luxurious funeral parlour! Open 10:00–18:00 Tuesday–Saturday; 13:00–18:00 Sunday.

Below: *The Metropolitan Museum's impressively spacious Sculpture Court is a place to sit and observe.*

Left: *Holbein's portrait of Sir Thomas More is just one of the Frick's gems.*

Whitney Museum of American Art ★

The Whitney Museum at 75th and Madison is uncompromisingly modern and filled with American art from Calder to De Kooning. The gift of Mrs Gertrude Vanderbilt Whitney, together with her large American collection, this museum is in a fiercely modern building. Look for work by Calder, Warhol, Pollock and O'Keeffe here. Open 11:00–18:00 Wednesday, Friday–Sunday; 13:00–20:00 Thursday.

Places of Worship ★

You don't have to be Jewish to appreciate the grandeur of Temple Emanuel-El, the biggest synagogue in the United States seating 2500. A brooding Romanesque structure, it's full of Eastern detail. You'll find it at Fifth Avenue and 65th. Also on the Upper East Side the onion domes of the Russian Orthodox Cathedral of St Nicholas adds a note of exoticism.

ACTIVITIES FOR CHILDREN

Aside from toy shops, choose the new-look **American Museum of Natural History** (Central Park West) with a parade of dinosaurs, exotic birds and lively programmes for children. Then there's the **Hayden Planetarium** with light shows next door. A visit to the Bronx Zoo with aerial rides is a good idea or discover Indians at the Brooklyn Museum. The Zoo and the Alice in Wonderland statue in Central Park or the Children's Garden and fountain at St John the Divine are good if it's a fine day.

8
Upper West Side

On the Upper West Side you are in a different world. It's the city's cultural suburb. Markedly removed from the Upper East Side across the park, it has its own way of life, attitudes and neighbourhoods that are more diverse and contrasted than almost anywhere else. You can find almost anything in the shops, and there's an overflow of movie houses, theatres and museums. The Upper West Side is comfortable, unassuming and straightforward, and your true West Ender wouldn't live anywhere else.

From West 59th Street, **Broadway** cleaves its way right up the middle – it's the Upper West Side's main street, with the subway just under the grassed median. On either side, it is lined with roomy old apartment buildings that extend down its side streets. There are a few rows of private houses (off **Amsterdam Avenue** and **Central Park West** and dotted along West End Avenue) but mostly it's given over to apartments. These range from narrow buildings on cross streets to the vast, many-floored residences along Central Park West with desirable leafy views. In fact, Central Park West is a parade of such buildings of which the **Dakota** (New York's first luxury apartment house) is best known, and still an exclusive address.

There's the **Lincoln Center** and the **Juilliard School**, the **American Museum of Natural History**, **Riverside Park** and **Fordham University**. Although there's plenty to see and do, the real reason for a visit is to see a genuine New York neighbourhood at work and at play.

DON'T MISS

*** Lincoln Center: the city's cultural playground.
** American Museum of Natural History: the natural world in a recently renovated building.
** Hayden Planetarium: see the stars and the astronomical shows.
** Riverside Park: fresh green turf by the Hudson.
* Central Park West: one of New York's stateliest thoroughfares.

Opposite: *Tall-towered Riverside Church, with an impressive carillon of bells, looms on the skyline.*

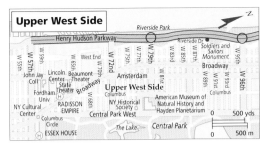

CULTURAL VENUES

The Upper West Side is no longer a cheap area so the writers, actors and musicians who live here tend to be well off. They come here to work and to settle and to maybe bring up a family. Since the originally run-down area went through a programme of urban renewal and became attractive in the 1950s, it's gained a sort of cachet. Together with the cultural developments and new university campuses like Fordham, it rapidly changed. Now along with the artists, white collar workers are also residents. The place is full of bookshops, art cinemas, smart shops and bars, new restaurants and theatres.

The Upper West Side's geographical spread of star sights is very much concentrated to the southeast, over to Central Park West. Many indeed are only a walk from the Park and spacious Lincoln Center or the green areas of Riverside Drive.

BOOKSHOPS IN THE CITY

New York has always been a book city with varied book shops, from grand stores such as the famous **Gotham Book Mart** near the Rockefeller Center to the multi-million volume **Strand** store in the East Village. The big firms have recently become even bigger. There are several along Broadway and these are veritable social centres, offering snack bars and sitting areas. They also stay open late at night and have become places to meet friends old and new.

Lincoln Center ★★★

This grandly ambitious gesture on the part of the city brought music, opera, dance and theatre together on one plaza in a central location. The Metropolitan Opera left its old location in Midtown to an airy space and a new and bigger house here on 62nd and Broadway.

The **Metropolitan Opera's** ('the Met's') new premises opened in 1966 and it's one of the smartest places to be seen at. Standing right at the focus of the Lincoln Center plaza, its high white arches give glimpses of the grand red-carpeted staircase and the

Chagall murals within. The oil company Texaco sponsors opera broadcasts and these are played over the airwaves to the nation on Saturday afternoons.

The Lincoln Center is regally flanked by **The New York State Theater**, home to the world-famous New York City Ballet and New York City Opera, and **Avery Fisher Hall**, home to the New York Philharmonic. Drama is housed at the **Vivian Beaumont Theater**. Also here is the **Dorothy and Lewis B. Cullman Center (New York Public Library for the Performing Arts)**, well worth a visit by theatre fans for its huge collection of theatre, dance, opera tapes, videos, manuscripts – and books.

The Lincoln Center is a handsome sight in pale marble grouped around a glimmering fountain. Between Avery Fisher Hall and the Juilliard are some modern sculptures, including a Henry Moore.

The Juilliard School of Music *

You can visit this school for professional musicians, singers and actors beside **Lincoln Center** for student performances, or recitals at the **Alice Tully Hall**. Some of America's best talents are nursed here. Aside from some of its alumni, it was briefly famous in the early 1970s when the great diva, Maria Callas, gave a short series of master-classes here.

Above: *The gleaming plaza and fountains of the Lincoln Center.*

Opposite: *The Met has more than 3000 seats for its opera and ballet seasons.*

OPERA IN NEW YORK

From the early days New York had its own opera house. The first was on the East Side near 14th Street, the second in grandiose style rose in Midtown. Not big enough to hold scenery and costumes for a repertory that changes daily, it was pulled down and replaced by an office building. Now called Golda Meir Square, its ghostly presence is commemorated by a pavement plaque at Broadway and 38th Street. The Met in Lincoln Center is one of the few places where a rotating repertory brings different operas every night.

ART DECO

Although originally a French style (Art Décoratif), the United States took to this style with enthusiasm in the 1920s. As such many buildings in Los Angeles, Seattle, Detroit, and Miami reflect this interest in the period. New York has some wonderful examples dotted around the city, and the Upper West Side has a selection along Central Park West's apartment row. Many buildings were constructed between the wars and some of them are impressive Art Deco *palazzi*.

WALKING ON THE WEST SIDE

To discover the Upper West Side, it would be a good idea to take a long walk up Central Park West beside the park and admire the often fantastic architecture of the palatial blocks of residential apartments. No. 1 is the **Hotel des Artistes**, a site where many stars have lodged. Stop to look at the **Dakota Apartments**, where many famous residents have had their New York headquarters. The film *Rosemary's Baby* was set in the Dakota and in 1980 John Lennon died here. His wife Yoko Ono created **Strawberry Fields** in the park opposite in his memory. It is now known as the Peace Park. The Dakota name, legend has it, came from the time it was built, so far out of New York's centre that 'you might as well be in Dakota'. At 77th Street is the city's oldest museum, the **New-York Historical Society**, with paintings, silver and glass and special shows.

American Museum of Natural History **

Set on Central Park West between 77th and 79th Streets, the largest natural history museum in the world has been undergoing massive renovation and given a new look. There are fascinating new, state-of-the art dinosaur halls, displays of animals living and extinct, ocean life, birds and all sorts of stones from gems to meteorites. It's a great place, and there are interesting live programmes and films too. Open 10:00–17:45, Mondays–Thursdays, Sunday; 10:00– 20:45 Friday and Saturday.

Below: *'Strawberry Fields' is a rare modern development in Central Park, and commemorates the work of John Lennon.*

Hayden Planetarium **

Adjoining the Natural History Museum is the exciting new Frederick Phineas and Sandra Priest Rose Center for Earth and Space, containing what is still generally called the Hayden Planetarium at 81st Street, where you can see magical views of the heavens. Both these museums are ideal for family visits. They are open 12:30–16:45 daily.

Note the shimmering Art Deco apartments at 90th Street, the **Eldorado**. Head up as far as West 96th Street, one of the main cross streets, and go west till you reach Broadway to see the **Symphony Space**, which is the headquarters for way-out new music. Then go over to the **Riverside Park** on the Hudson side.

Above: *Zabar's isn't just a famed Jewish delicatessen and bakery. It's a New York institution.*

Riverside Drive and Park **

This broad green area, hilly and wooded, stretches from 72nd to 145th Street and was designed by Frederic Law Olmsted, one of Central Park's creators.

Cross over on 86th Street, with its churches, in order to go down Broadway. The **Children's Museum of Manhattan** is on 83rd Street off Broadway. It is a fascinating experience for children, where they learn through play. There is a multimedia show and hi-tech equipment is available. Also, at various locations around here you will find all sorts of ethnic food and wine shops, as well as open fruit and vegetable stalls.

Small parks along Broadway commemorate the composer, Verdi (at 72nd) and the philosopher, Dante (at 63rd). The **American Bible Society** on West 62nd will appeal to those who are interested in the Good Book. If Art Deco fascinates you, then don't miss the sculpted façade of 1845 Broadway, which was once a garage and is now offices. Just down Broadway from here is **Columbus Circle**, where you will find exhibition halls and a cluster of big hotels. The Circle is also the gateway to the Upper West Side.

WEST SIDE EATING

Eating out poses no problems here, with a host of restaurants of all ethnic persuasions. But perhaps best of all is the array of shops offering tantalizing snacks and takeaway foods: from imported coffees to cakes there's everything here. Many offer Jewish specialities. The famous Zabar's has many kinds of bread, as well as delicatessen items and it's usually stuffed full with people buying their favourite, be it hard dark rye or zesty poppy seed rolls.

9
Harlem and
Washington Heights

Despite its poor image, Harlem isn't all that bad and there is much of this stretch of Upper Manhattan that is worth seeing, especially for the discerning tourist and one interested in the history of the city. Harlem was the first stop for many blacks who were escaping slavery and persecution in the South. From the early years of this century they arrived from all over, and to this day continue to do so. Harlem can be slummy, rundown and terrifyingly poor, yet it conceals some surprising islands of wealth as well as several historic spots.

The Harlem high street is **125th Street**, cutting right through the district and with all kinds of life and at all hours. East Harlem, from 110th Street up about 30 blocks, has been El Barrio, or **Spanish Harlem** since Puerto Ricans began arriving here several decades ago. The best and safest way to see this area is to take a guided tour. These include visits to hear and see choirs at gospel churches. A notable Harlem restaurant is Sylvia's where you can try the tasty 'soul food'.

Columbia University occupies a site at the edge of Harlem from 114th to 121st streets. This is Ivy League New York, and its neighbour is **Barnard College**. At the edge of **Morningside Park** is the vast, unfinished **Cathedral of St John the Divine**.

North of Harlem, **Washington Heights** is now a great mixture of peoples and cultures. The **George Washington Bridge** spans the Hudson River here, and north along Fort Washington Avenue is the delightful **Fort Tryon Park** and the **Cloisters Museum**.

DON'T MISS

*** **The Cloisters:** medieval marvels from the Metropolitan Museum.
** **Cathedral of St John the Divine:** New York's mammoth Anglican cathedral.
* **A tour of Harlem:** the best way to see black New York.
* **Columbia University:** New York's Ivy League college.
* **George Washington Bridge:** a huge yet delicate suspension bridge.

Opposite: *An extraordinary mixture, Harlem is a place where you can try soul food – or buy a used police car!*

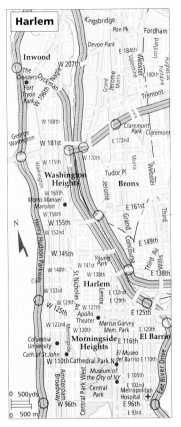

AROUND 125TH STREET

The heart of Harlem is the middle slice of 125th Street. This continuously busy street is also known as the **Martin Luther King Jr Boulevard** and there are many bars, clubs and fast-food spots. Here also is the famous **Apollo Theater**, alive and bright again and achieving a comeback; the **Studio Museum** and the **Harlem Third World Trade Center**. The one-time Teresa Hotel at Seventh Avenue and 125th was the site for Fidel Castro to address Harlem (unofficially) from a balcony.

Harlem is neither as bad nor as grim as it is often depicted, but its image holds it back. It's certainly impoverished, with many broken-down houses and grim streets. Yet, poor as it is, it is also culturally rich and it was for many escaping black slaves, a promised land, a place to settle and live decently. In reality, though, Harlem has some of the worst slums in the nation. Today, along with **El Barrio** it's home to half a million poor blacks and Puerto Ricans.

In the 1920s during Prohibition, Harlem was *the* place to visit, and music and song flourished at its clubs. The stars were there, and so were numerous jazz clubs and cabarets. **The Cotton Club** was the most famous, and with the **Apollo Theater**, it led the way. The Apollo has been refurbished and still presents popular talent nights – over the years it has launched many stars into the international firmament.

Although it's easy to get to 125th Street, many people don't like to visit Harlem alone. To see Harlem easily, take a tour with an experienced operator. This way you'll be comfortably transported to see places such as **Hamilton Grange**, the **Morris-Jumel Mansion**, **Striver's Row**, **Audubon Terrace**, **Boricua College** and the enchanting **Aunt Len's Doll and Toy Museum**, a collection of over 5000 dolls set up by a retired schoolteacher.

Opposite above:

A typical Lennox Avenue street scene with the austere Malcolm X building acting as backdrop.

HARLEM'S HIGH TIME

They came from all over to perform at the Cotton Club. The music was blues and jazz, and the stars of the 1920s were Fats Waller, Jellyroll Morton, Billie Holliday, Charlie Parker, Bessie Smith, Charlie Mingus. The list goes on and on. Here, inventive music met memorable singers, and a new style was born. Wealthy New Yorkers came to hear the new music and to drink. During Prohibition and the Depression, Harlem certainly kept its spirits up.

Spanish Harlem

This quarter runs from the northeast edge of Central Park above 110th Street and along to the East River (which at this point becomes the Harlem River). **El Barrio**, as it's called, or **The Neighbourhood**, is a place that resounds with noise and abounds with low-life. Its main stem is 116th Street, and there are many stalls and local foods to be sampled and savoured. Unfortunately it is a drug domain, so visit by day and take care. Don't stray off the main streets.

Museo del Barrio *

Below 110th Street it is safer and this is where, at Fifth Avenue and 104th, you will find the Museo del Barrio. This is a museum dedicated to the arts of Latin

HARLEM TOURS

For a glimpse of the famous Harlem gospel singing, take a tour from **Harlem Spirituals Inc** at 1457 Broadway. Other possible itineraries include visits to historic houses or a Baptist service. Tours go from 1697 Broadway at 53rd Street. Another group, **Harlem Renaissance Tours**, operates with the Gray Line. It features visits to famous spots and gospel singing at a Harlem church and starts from the Gray Line depot at Eighth Avenue and 54th Street. **Penny Sightseeing Company** has walking tours and also includes a visit to a church to hear gospel singing.

Left: *A flower seller selling his wares in the cluttered streets and markets of Spanish Harlem.*

WONDERS AT THE CLOISTERS

Here you can see a remarkable collection of medieval art from the Metropolitan Museum's overflowing vaults. The treasures range from illuminated manuscripts to the fabled Unicorn Tapestries. This is an experience not to be missed. In between the galleries are gardens containing sculptures, and the atmosphere is as calm and serene as the era it shows.

America and Puerto Rico and there is a changing and lively programme. There is also a permanent collection of interesting pre-Columbian artefacts. Open 11:00–17:00 Wednesday–Sunday.

Columbia University *

Founded in the 18th century, this is a member of the prestigous Ivy League colleges. It spreads between Amsterdam Avenue and Broadway from 114th Street. There are three undergraduate schools with over 18,000 students. The campus is essentially an urban one, yet still spacious and with some handsome 19th-century buildings. Among them is the impressive Low Library, a few modern buildings as well as the colonnaded Butler Library. Nearby, Barnard College, beyond Broadway, is worth an exploratory walk. Tours can be arranged.

Cathedral of St John the Divine ***

Beside Morningside Park, this huge cathedral is situated at 112th Street and Amsterdam Avenue. It dominates the neighbourhood, and this Gothic edifice shouldn't be missed. As New York's Anglican cathedral, it is reputedly bigger than Notre Dame and Chartres and, although begun in 1892 and having survived changes of style, it's still not finished. There are several attractions within, from an ancient fossil to an altar dedicated to AIDS victims. Open 07:00–17:00, Monday–Sunday.

Below: *The AIDS Memorial can be seen in its own chapel at St John the Divine Cathedral.*

A fascinating place to visit on weekdays is the studio where the masons and sculptors work on the pieces needed to construct and decorate the building. The cathedral is being built on traditional lines and the masons can be seen at work in the **Stonecutting Yard** (Monday–Friday). Many works of art have been given to the Anglican cathedral and can be seen on a rotating basis in its museum.

WASHINGTON HEIGHTS

A huddle of apartment buildings and crowded streets, with many discount outlets and bargain stores, Washington Heights stretches north from 155th Street. This once-Irish enclave is now a great ethnic mix. It's also an area where you can taste unusual foods. Although it is becoming trendier, it still has a drug problem and, apart from cheap shopping, there's not much to tempt the tourist.

Above: *Under the double decks of the George Washington Bridge is an historic fort and a landmark: the Little Red Lighthouse.*

At 178th Street is the George Washington Bridge Bus Station and, in the shadow of the bridge itself, is **Fort Washington Park**, where a few remains of the original fort can be seen.

The Cloisters Museum ***

Fort Tryon Park is another of Frederick Law Olmsted's creations and has at its centrepiece old **Fort Tryon** which saw service in the War of Independence. But most famous is the museum, **The Cloisters**. Here, in elegant and cool surroundings, are medieval treasures from the Metropolitan Museum of Art. It's a wonderful collection and is easily reached by subway to 190th Street followed by a pleasant walk through the park. You can also take a direct bus from the Met itself on Fifth Avenue.

The building appears to be an authentic 13th-century edifice, but is actually comprised of bits of old French and Spanish monasteries. Open 09:30–17:15 Tuesday–Sunday (16:45 in winter).

George Washington Bridge *

Arching high over the Hudson River, this 14-lane, two-levelled suspension bridge crossing to the Jersey Heights is particularly impressive at night. From the Palisade Parkway on the other shore you get an equally good view, including Manhattan's lights.

ACTIVITIES AT THE CATHEDRAL

St John's has a busy schedule of secular events, and there are bound to be theatre or dance performances and exhibitions when you visit. It's a lively place, and a concert is a lovely experience. In the neighbouring **Children's Sculpture Garden** is a curious fountain and works by local schoolchildren.

10
Beyond Manhattan

Inland and up and down the Eastern Seaboard there are many interesting places that will make an ideal day or half day out, be it a country tour, a trip to a beach, a theme park, or an historic town. Aside from the other four boroughs, all clustering close around Manhattan and which can be visited by bus or subway, the city has a wonderful range of parks and beaches of its own. Check with the tourist office or, if driving, follow local indications.

Other destinations offer many choices for days out by coach, self-drive car or train beyond the reach of local transport, into **New York State**, up into **Connecticut** or across into **New Jersey**. All three states have surprising countryside and tourist attractions of their own.

The Long Island Railroad will take you to the torpedo-shaped island that angles off Manhattan, its southern 'toe' occupied by **Brooklyn** and **Queens**. Go further and **Long Island** gets really rural, with some of the most beautiful and wildest beaches and rugged and unspoilt countryside. Alternatively, you could use the same service to go to Connecticut, which has a long seashore. Also, beyond the commuter fringe and cluttered shore strip in the south, is very pretty wooded country.

There is a variety of things to do beyond the borders of the city and a wide range of places to visit, all within a short distance. The various tourist boards will happily assist you. Be sure to ask about bargain day-out fares as well as the special offers on coaches.

DON'T MISS

*** Bronx Zoo: with the Botanical Gardens – a real New York surprise.
** Circle Line Cruise: the best way to see the city – from the water.
** Long Island: New York's seaside and country.
** Hudson River Valley: a day trip for scenic beauty.
** Staten Island: once off the ferry, a place for discovery.
* Princeton, New Jersey: a charming and photogenic university town.

Opposite: *A handsome Colonial house with pillars and porticoes at Renselaerville.*

Above: *The Brooklyn Botanic Garden is fenced with suburban houses, and though small is worth a visit.*

Opposite: *The Queens' Dockland, East River, is a cluttered part of the inlet leading to Harlem River.*

BROOKLYN AND QUEENS

A cursory glance might not reveal much of interest in the two boroughs that lie side by side on the end of Long Island. The only bit of **Brooklyn** and **Queens** many people see is the drive in from **Kennedy Airport** and much of it is suburban sprawl. But don't dismiss it as worthless views of endless huddled housing interspersed with the occasional park. These two boroughs do have some surprising things to discover, particularly Brooklyn.

Brooklyn was once its own city with a good deal of civic pride. If it had not been absorbed into **Greater New York** in 1898, it would now be one of the biggest cities in the United States. This is evidenced by its many civic attractions, concert halls and seats of learning, the grandiose buildings at its centre and by still-smart suburbs such as **Brooklyn Heights**. There's a sense of history too – the colony on the bluff was founded by the Dutch 350 years ago. They named it *Breuckelen* and, except for a dip into decline in the 1950s, it has remained a delightful place to live and visit. With its handsome terrace houses and harbour views, it is now a designated Historic District.

You can easily reach the Heights on its cliffs by subway, downtown bridges or through the 2 mile-long (4km) **Brooklyn Battery Tunnel**, the longest road tunnel in the country.

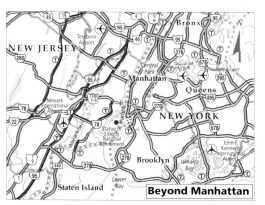

Beyond Manhattan

Brooklyn Museum **

Consider also a visit to the Brooklyn Museum, a treasure house and one of the biggest museums in the entire country, with large collections of primitive artefacts of American Indian, African and Pacific arts. There's a fascinating hoard of things to see, from 18th-century colonial furniture and European paintings to Egyptology and ancient Assyrian sculpture. There's also a mock-up of a 17th-century Dutch house with authentic furnishings, a costume centre and works by local artists of the Hudson River School.

The museum is located by the **Brooklyn Botanic Garden** on the Eastern Parkway which, although small, has specialist gardens and collections, and large conservatories. The borough is also home to the **New York Aquarium**.

There are many shows that come into the **Brooklyn Academy**, a short subway journey from Manhattan. This is a grand old Victorian theatre with smaller stages and is a good place to catch up with unusual dance and theatre pieces.

Brooklyn may have the bigger population, but **Queens** is the largest borough in the area. It has several sporting facilities, including **Shea Stadium** and **Aqueduct Race Track,** and both the major New York airports, **LaGuardia** and **Kennedy**, are here.

Below: *Yankee Stadium. Home of the famous Yankee baseball stars, the big bowl is crowded for every game of the season.*

THE BRONX AND STATEN ISLAND

Amidst the dispiriting grimness of the Bronx is the **Bronx Botanical Garden** and the **Zoo** – a wondrous place indeed. This contiguous spread of 500 acres (202ha) is easily reached by subway to Pelham Parkway. The two attractions are neighbours yet separate.

Yankee Stadium *

The local baseball teams are the Mets and the New York Yankees, and games are played in the April to October summer season. The Yankees meet at the vast Yankee Stadium at 161st Street. Tickets can be hard to come by. If you have contacts with seasoned subscribers, ask them.

Bronx Zoo and International Wildlife Park ***

This is a winner; a century old, yet kept well up to date with a collection of several thousand animals, reptiles and birds, shown in large spaces that are made to be as natural as possible. All six continents are represented. There's a World of Darkness show for nocturnal animals and a children's zoo. However, some of the open exhibits are closed in winter. Open 10:00–17:00 daily.

Next door and to the north is the **New York Botanical Gardens** with glades of azalea and rhododendron, as well as many native American plants and trees. The elegant Enid A Haupt Conservatory contains interesting tropical plants. Best times for visiting are early spring through summer. Open 10:00–18:00 Tuesday–Sunday.

Van Cortland Mansion *

A visit to a country house in the Bronx sounds a bit strange, yet here in the midst of it off 242nd Street is the **Van Cortland Mansion**. Unpretentious, it still stands in its park, now mostly put to

Left: *In the Richmond Settlement on Staten Island you feel as if you're in a country town.*

use as playing fields. This 18th-century country house was a headquarters for General Washington during the struggle for independence. Although its name suggests a Dutch origin, it's really a simple Georgian stone mansion. Recently restored in its protected setting, it has a fine collection of period china and furniture and a few rooms are open to the public. Open 10:00–15:00 Tuesday–Friday, 11:00–16:00 Saturday and Sunday.

Staten Island **

Your journeys of discovery round New York don't have to be exclusively on the road or the underground. You can go by boat and anyway you can only get to Staten Island from Manhattan by ferry. And what a trip! If the weather is fine you can spend half a day or more on Staten Island and take the ferry from the Battery in Lower Manhattan. The journey across the harbour adds considerably to the fun. Staten Island is part of **Richmond**, a surprisingly large borough offering views of Lower Manhattan, Ellis Island and the Statue of Liberty and an introduction to the city's busy harbour as well. Here you can find several interesting things to see, including **Historic Richmond Town** (a restored example of an early New York village), the historic **Snug Harbour Cultural Center** and the **Jacques Marchais Center of Tibetan Art**.

CRUISING AROUND THE CITY

Aside from the famous ferry, you can make the best of fine weather by taking regular cruises to discover, or circumnavigate, Manhattan Island, or simply enjoy an evening of dancing and drinking. New York is a city on the water and outings go from several points. The **Circle Line Cruises** depart from berths at Pier 83, West 42nd Street. If you would like a more formal trip with dinner, there's the **World Yacht** which goes from Pier 81 and gives a lunch, brunch or dinner excursion. From Lower Manhattan's Pier 16 you can sail the harbour on **Seaport Liberty Cruises.** This one sails regularly from South Street Seaport in Lower Manhattan, and most will have live musical entertainment.

Above: *Where the wealthy play – yachts in the Sound off Long Island.*
Opposite: *Fire Island is a line of sand protecting Long Island from the Atlantic Ocean. There are superb beaches here.*

LONG ISLAND COUNTRY

Inland Long Island is often overlooked, yet its country pleasures are delightful. Rural roads, sea views, little restaurants offering local seafood such as the delicious tiny Bay Scallops. Try them broiled in butter. Small farms grow potatoes, corn and vegetables; there are lots of roadside stands in season to sell you fresh produce for picnics. You'll find plenty of quiet places for alfresco meals too.

LONG ISLAND **

New York is a marvellous place for a holiday but don't forget that the city, with its complex web of transport, both local and long distance, is also perfect as a base for the discovery of other cities, out-of-town sites and local centres of attraction. Long Island is a case in point. This huge piece of land, over 200 miles (320km) long, extends to the Atlantic and is essentially rural once you leave the New York suburbs. Trains depart from **Pennsylvania Station** (also known as Penn Station) but can be crowded at certain times of the day because they serve so many commuters.

You'll discover an undulating landscape that becomes more and more countrified as you go further northeast, with small settlements and neat farms. Trains are slow and the carriages are hardly modern, yet you get the best view this way: if you drive a hire-car you may find it hard to navigate and on the elevated highways your views will be mostly of other cars!

The **Long Island Railroad** will give you a real taste of the island, from pastures to open sea. Especially popular in summer, it will also take you to a number of resorts along the east coast as well as commuter suburbs.

Beaches

There are beaches all around the island, but those facing the open sea are peerless wide stretches of white sand. Lapped by the Atlantic, with long, cleansing rollers, the shore is a perfect destination even out of season, but wonderful on a hot summer day. At weekends, though, the parks and beaches may be very crowded with New Yorkers bent on escaping the city heat. It's a good idea to take a picnic and to use the barbecue facilities offered in the state parks. There are many of these facilities and they are free.

The train stops at ferry points for the thin spit of sandy land known as **Fire Island**, a very popular destination in summer, dotted with resorts for every taste. The 40-odd summer settlements are connected by walkways and cater for families, singles and gay people. Fire Island is a long sandbar protecting the east coast of the island, home to small parks and a chain of seaside resorts and the beaches are wide and clean.

About two hours along the coast are the resorts known as **The Hamptons** – the neat little towns of Westhampton, South and Easthampton, the latter pair wildly chic in summer, expensive and filled with New Yorkers on vacation. It's as if the entire Upper East Side had flown out like exotic birds to perch here in cool summer cottages. You can continue further to the remote end of Long Island and **Amagansett**, which is where the rich and the less flamboyant have summer houses to get away from it all. The sands are wide, the sky and sea views huge and the beaches are often deserted. If you want an experience of peace then it is advisable to come out of season.

CONEY ISLAND

Once a lively amusement park, Coney Island has seen better times. Now it is a sad shadow of its former great days and many guide books don't even mention it. It sits at the end of a subway line on a wide, polluted beach yet it still offers fairground lures. Here, you'll find the New York Aquarium, Little Russia with its shops and cafés at Brighton Beach, and also a New York label for hot dogs – Nathan's Famous – where you must take the family for American frankfurters and fries.

Above: *The view of Lower Manhattan as you arrive from across the Hudson in New Jersey.*

POLITICAL JOKERS

Atlantic City has seen several political jamborees. At the time when Barry Goldwater was made the Republican's presidential candidate in the 1960s, a billboard image of the ultra-Conservative senator was highly visible as you entered the town. 'In your heart you know he's right' trumpeted the slogan. This was fine until someone scrawled, 'yeah, extreme right' across the poster and rather spoiled it for Atlantic City.

NEW JERSEY

To the west is New Jersey, which is not as grim and grey as some of its eastern parts would indicate. From the bluffs of the Hudson River just across the George Washington Bridge you get fine views of Manhattan from the Palisade's Parkway. Newark is being improved, and shiny black office buildings rise over Mulberry Fishmarket.

Princeton *

An hour's train journey will take you to Princeton, another Ivy League university which is highly recommended for a day trip. This is an elegant small university town with a campus that's all in approved stone Gothic style. Friendly and photogenic, there are pretty white-fenced streets and clapboard houses.

Even the rich repository of arts and architecture and the city of Brotherly Love, **Philadelphia**, in the state of Pennsylvania, is only a 90-minute bus journey away.

Depressingly ugly Hoboken, Jersey City and Elizabeth may be, with their heavy industry and run-down houses, but they are not typical. Get beyond them and you will find pretty countryside and in the west, some smart 'hunting country'. With its northern towns very much sleeper suburbs for New York, its southern extremities very rural and even empty, New Jersey is a state of contrasts.

It has some very fine country but you'll need to allow time to discover it. In the far west is the lovely **Delaware Water Gap** along the wide river valley – drive and enjoy the small settlements and wonderful old inns on the Delaware banks, and New Jersey towns like **Flemington** and **Lambertville**. At this town you can cross into Pennsylvania and the town of **New Hope** which is the centre for the beautifully rustic Bucks County.

Atlantic City *

The sea coast of New Jersey, with wild country and wonderful extensive beaches, is a world away from Long Island, although in its long sweep from New York's harbour to the lonely country of **Cape May**, it has attractive seaside communities. The major one gained immense favour in the early part of the 20th century as a getaway place for New Yorkers. This is Atlantic City, with its famous attractions and sandy beaches.

Atlantic City reached a high-water mark in the 1920s (evoked in the musical *42nd Street*), but since then has declined in fashion. It's had its great moments, and continues to host major meetings and the occasional big party conference. The city still has the usual seaside attractions plus casino and sports some lures such as the famous wooden boardwalk that runs along the promenade above the beach and was the place to be seen 75 years ago when Atlantic City was smart and popular. The town has had to revamp itself, but its old hotels have character and charm.

THE PORT AUTHORITY BUS TERMINAL

A very important link for coach and bus travel, the terminal is a 24-hour operation. You can cross America from here – or take coaches to the three city airports. Clean, well-ordered and safe, it has good cafés and bars.

Below: *Atlantic City used to be a fashionable resort for New Yorkers. Now it's famed for its casinos.*

Below: *Litchfield,
Connecticut is a quiet place
and here you will see typical
wooded country houses.*

CONNECTICUT

A little further to the north from New York, is **New England**. This area of six states has much to offer and two of them are within easy reach of New York. The most southerly of the six is Connecticut.

You can get to **New Haven** by bus or train. It's a comfortable town which was first laid out in the 17th century. New Haven has fine museums and three early churches at its centre. It is also the home of **Yale**, another member of the Ivy League club, and guided tours leave from Phelps Gate. You could visit the state capital, **Hartford**, which has a handsome state capitol building and connections with the 19th-century novelists Mark Twain and Harriet Beecher-Stowe. You can even go as far as Providence to discover the state of **Rhode Island** and **Newport** with its palatial summer houses built for the New York rich with the French chateau in mind. These destinations would be served better with a night's stopover in order to avoid having a frustratingly short stay.

Connecticut itself has a string of beaches along its ocean shore. If you can get as far as **Mystic** you'll discover an old whaling station and a maritime museum where craftsmen display old sea-going skills. Nearby **New London** is a lively place with a deep harbour and associations with the writer Eugene O'Neill.

Connecticut is also very rural once you have got over its southern commuter belt. It has small farms and old-style towns and villages. Some are typically New England with quite a different character in its residents. If you only have time for one or two then consider **Litchfield** or **Wethersfield**, both with a wealth of Colonial houses.

Left: *Along the Hudson River little streams join the broad river in its stately valley.*
Overleaf: *It is hard to imagine that the South Street Seaport once dominated the river. Now the Financial District dwarfs it.*

LOWER NEW YORK STATE

New York is actually a huge state with many attractions, but such lures as **Lake Champlain**, the **Finger Lakes**, **Rochester** and the **Ontario shore** are too far for day trips. The southern part of the state has much to offer, though, and it's charmingly low-key and agreeable.

A drive along the **Hudson River Valley** from New York has many pleasures and a host of small state and historic parks to visit. Stop at **West Point Military Academy**, for its museum and visitor centre, or scan the views from **Bear Mountain**. Stately homes, American style, are the **Vanderbilt Mansion**, **Mills Mansion** and **Hyde Park**, the Springwood estate of Franklin D Roosevelt. These beautiful homes are to be found in the neighbourhood of **Poughkeepsie**, once the state capital. At the present state capital of **Albany** there's much to take in too. Another beautifully rural drive can be followed through the **Catskill Mountains**, where Washington Irving's fictional character Rip Van Winkle fell asleep.

New York City At a Glance

BEST TIMES TO VISIT

Most times of the year, except high summer (July and August) when it's often hot and uncomfortably humid. In winter it can be sharply cold and frosty, but dry. As New York is on the same latitude as Spain, dusk does not come too early. Best periods are from **April –June** (spring) when the weather is balmy and **September–October** when autumn weather is crisp yet warm. Families celebrate during Thanksgiving (end of November) and Christmas (when you may get considerable snowfalls) but New York makes up for it by being festive and fun.

GETTING THERE

New York is one of the best connected cities in the world. It's served by most airlines from all major world cities, often with direct flights. There is a choice of three airports and, while **JF Kennedy** and **Newark** handle most of the international flights, **LaGuardia** is usually for domestic services. You can also arrive by ship on occasional trans-Atlantic sailings direct to the West Side docks from Europe, notably the QE2. There are services by train from the US cities that still have rail connections. **Greyhound** bus and other coach companies depart from all US and Canadian

points, and some Mexican ones too. If you plan to see New York City as part of an Eastern Seaboard tour you can rent **cars** easily from a big selection of rental agencies in town and at all airports. You may be charged a fee to drop them off at a different destination from the pickup point. Take out full insurance. Gas (petrol) is very cheap.

GETTING AROUND

There is a very good public transport system, although some people are put off at the thought of descending into the **subway**. Don't be. The subway is safe except late at night when it's less used. It's been cleaned up, and well-policed over recent years. It runs for 24 hours, it's efficient, cheap and very fast, especially between express stops. The subway extends all over the city except Richmond (Staten Island) and New Jersey. A separate system called **PATH** brings commuters in under the Hudson from Jersey City.

The **subway map**, obtainable at every station or from information booths, is a bit confusing for visitors and you may need help in working out which train to take and where you get off and transfer. Buy tokens for a flat price fare all over the centre at subway booths. These can also be used on buses, which

operate principally along main avenues. These can be slow at rush hour. The Metrocard, a magnetic farecard, can also be used on subways and, within New York City, on all public and most private buses, with a free transfer between subway and buses. Private coach services link the airports to the **Port Authority Bus Terminal** on Eighth Avenue, or the 42nd Street entrance of **Grand Central Terminal**. The subway (Eighth Avenue A Express train, same as the city flat fare) also links Kennedy Airport with frequent **airport shuttle bus services** which go to all the airline terminals and are free. **Taxis:** Yellow cabs are to be hailed anywhere at any time, and they are frequent and reasonable. You can rent **bicycles** at certain points (a good way to encompass Central Park) and some younger visitors even glide around town on **skates** or **rollerblades**. **Walking** is also easy and direct, since almost all streets go from east to west and avenues from north to south, and it's certainly safe on busy main roads in central Manhattan. **Suburban Trains:** Port Authority Trans-Hudson (PATH) operates 4 lines to and from New Jersey with connections at Hoboken and Newark to NJ Transit. Information toll-free, tel:

New York City At a Glance

(212) 800 234-7284.
Metro-North goes from
Grand Central to the northern suburbs and Connecticut, tel: (212) 352-4900.
The **Long Island Railroad**
goes to the island from
Pennsylvania Station, tel:
(212) 718 217-5477. **Penn
Station** also serves with
Amtrak cities beyond New
York that have rail
connections. Information
from the **Metropolitan
Transit Authority**, tel:
(212) 718 330-1234,
24 hour daily service.

WHERE TO STAY

Many possibilities exist in a
range of prices, from **hostels**
and **bed-and-breakfasts** to
motels and top luxury hotels.
It's unlikely that most visitors
will want to stay anywhere
other than in the centre, so
the following are almost all
Manhattan-based suggestions,
and since there are so many,
this is only a short representative list of possibilities. More
detailed lists can be found at
CitySearch, at http://www.
newyork.citysearch.com
Consider using a booking service: room reservations can be
made with **Accommodations
Express**, a free service which
can get you discounts in a
range of New York City hotels.
Call (800) 444-7666 for this
seven-day a week service. If
you are going to visit the city
for a weekend you will find
that many **hotels** will compete

to offer lower rates when
business people have gone
home. Check the newspapers,
particularly the *New York
Times* or the **New York
Convention and Visitors'
Bureau** (810 Seventh Avenue,
NY 10019) for bargain weekend packages, or ask hotels
when booking direct. Packages can also include tours,
free meals, plus all those little
extra luxuries to invite you in
to fill rooms at quiet times.
Bear in mind that the price
quoted will not usually include
the steep local NYC taxes.
These may well add 20%
and more to your bill. Note
that Manhattan telephone
numbers are all prefixed 212,
if calling long distance, but
beyond the island they differ.
Another option is **Homestay
New York**, a well-respected
accommodation service for
those who want the experience of living with real New
Yorkers. Hosts are carefully
screened and matched with
guests. Visit their website at
www.homestayny.com

Midtown
LUXURY
The Essex House, on Central
Park West with another
entrance on 58th Street. 160
Central Park South, tel: (212)
247-0300, fax: 315-1839. An
old hotel of impeccable style.
Excellent service and two
notable restaurants.The hotel
offers a wonderful health spa
and a business centre.

The Four Seasons, East 57th
Street. Notable restaurant,
57 East 57th Street, tel: (212)
758-5700, fax: 758-5711.
New York's newest, grandest
and biggest. Tall too, with
huge foyers, large rooms and
all-round views of the city. A
smart address on the East Side.

The Plaza, Fifth Ave, at 59th
Street, tel: (212) 759-3000,
fax: 759-3167. Perhaps New
York's most famous hotel,
facing Central Park and Fifth
Avenue. It's expensive, a
grande dame of a place and
bars like the Oak Room are
smart places for meetings.

UN Plaza, 44th at First
Avenue, tel: (212) 758-1234,
fax: 702-5051.You can have
an unusual experience here –
play tennis and swim indoors,
high up in the air and with
views of the UN Building too!

**The Sheraton New York
Tower**, 811 Seventh
Avenue, tel: (212) 581-1000,
fax 262-4410. Very handy for
Broadway theatres, this
huge, modern hotel is the
smart place for Happy Hour
drinks in their Tower Lounge.

Waldorf-Astoria, 301 Park
Ave, tel: (212) 355-3000,
fax: 759-9209. On posh
Park Avenue, this hotel's
old-style grandeur attracts
the rich and famous.
Elaborately gilded Art Deco
style everywhere.

New York City At a Glance

MID-RANGE
The Algonquin Hotel,
59 West 44th. Very central,
tel: (212) 840-6800, fax:
944-1419. A famous hotel if
literature is your interest. Old
style, rather alluring with a
dark panelled lounge at its
entrance where you can get
a drink or tea.

Paramount, 235 West 46th
Street, tel: (212) 764-5500,
fax: 575-4892. Stylishly
remodelled in faddy-fifties
style, yet maintaining its
1920s atmosphere, this hotel
is popular with young business people and arty types.
Rooms tend to be small, but
it's very handy for Broadway.

Radisson Empire, 44 West
63rd Street, tel: (212) 265-
7400, fax: 315-0349. At
Columbus Circle, Lincoln
Center. Modern, welcoming.
The Radisson-SAS group has
several good city hotels, and
look out for ones in New
Jersey for bargain stays.

**Mayflower Hotel on the
Park**, 15 Central Park West,
tel: (212) 265-0060, fax:
265-5098. A large hotel facing the park combining an
old-style welcome with in-
room pantries and refrigera-
tors. Fitness centre. Close to
subways, West Side restaurants and shopping.

Wellington Hotel, 871
Seventh Ave, tel: (212) 247-

3900, fax: 581-1719. Good
value, near to Broadway
showplaces. A 1930s sur-
vivor, it also has a coffee
shop and cocktail bar.

BUDGET
Gramercy Park Hotel, 2
Lexington Ave, tel: (212)
475-4320, fax: 505-0535.
Despite its smart townhouse
aspect this small hotel is
reasonable and has desirable
park-facing rooms – you also
get access to this rare green
enclave.

Pickwick Arms, 230 East
51st, tel: (212) 355-0300,
fax: 755-5029. Bigger than it
looks, this is a reasonably
priced place if you want
economy in midtown.
There's also a roof garden
and a bar available.

Stanford Hotel, 43 West
32nd, tel: (212) 563-1500,
fax: 629-0043. A small hotel
that offers low prices for
those on a budget and is
neat and central. Well-placed
for the shops at Herald
Square as well as for visiting
the Javits Convention Center.

Aladdin Hotel, 317 West
45th Street, tel: (212) 977-
5700, fax: 246-6036.
Recently renovated and cen-
trally located, this is a bargain option for those who
don't mind shared bath-
rooms and dormitory-style
sleeping accomodation.

Vanderbilt YMCA,
224 East 47th Street,
tel: (212) 755-2410.
Despite the name both
sexes can stop off here. This
recently renovated hostel is
in the heart of midtown east,
has plenty of sports facilities
and is close to the UN.

NY Student Center/YMCA,
356 West 34th Street, tel:
(212) 760-5850. William
Sloane House: This huge hostel is grim and forbidding in
a dreary part of town but it
offers bargain accommoda-
tion and there's a 24-hour
policing of corridors. Takes
regular visitors and students.

**New York Bed and
Breakfast** does exist, and at
a price you can stay with the
genuine New Yorkers in their
own homes. Try the following but be sure to check
ahead of time of arrival.

Bed and Breakfast Bureau,
330 West 42nd Street, tel:
(212) 957-9786.

**City Lights Bed and
Breakfast Ltd**, PO Box
20355, Cherokee Station,
NYC, NY 10028, tel: (212)
737-8251.

**New World Bed and
Breakfast**, 150 Fifth
Avenue, no. 711, 10011, tel:
toll free (800) 443-3800 – in
USA and Canada, otherwise
the number is 675-5600.

New York City At a Glance

Uptown
LUXURY
The Carlyle,
35 East 76th Street,
tel: (212) 744-1600,
fax: 717-4682. A fine
historic hotel in notable
Art Deco style. This is a place
that has a choosy clientele
who like to be close to
museums and the Madison
Avenue sales-rooms
and smart shops.

Lowell Hotel,
28 East 63rd,
tel: (212) 838-1400,
fax: 319-4230. If you yearn
for old-world comforts
(even open fires in some
rooms) and are willing to
pay the price for high quality
New York accommodation,
this is a gem. It also has
a very good restaurant.

The Mark,
25 East 77th Street,
tel: (212) 744-4300,
fax: 744-2749. An elegant
hotel on the Upper East Side
close to the park and the
Metropolitan Museum.
Old style European service
and a club-like informal
restaurant in the foyer.

BUDGET
**International Student
Center**, 38 West 88th Street,
it is close to Central Park,
tel: (212) 787-7706.
You won't meet any
Americans here – it's only
open to foreigners, mostly

students. It feels like old New
York, a mansion house on
a leafy street but there are
dormitory rooms inside.

**New York YHA
International Hostel**,
891 Amsterdam Avenue,
tel: (212) 932-2300. High
on the Upper West Side
this very large hostel is well
looked after, offers real bargain rates, varied services
and has a lovely garden.

West Side YMCA, it is
just off Central Park at
5 West 63rd Street,
tel: (212) 787- 4400.
Well-equipped if a little
bit severe in style, this
hostel has been very well
renovated and offers bargain
rooms with lots of good
sport choices including
an indoor running track.

Downtown
LUXURY
Millennium Hilton,
55 Church Street, tel: (212)
693-2001, fax: 571-2317.
If you want to be right
downtown and lapped in
modern luxury, this new
hotel by the World Trade
Center is an idea, has great
views and with facilities
for the business visitor.

**Marriot World Trade
Center**, 3 WTC, tel: (212)
938-9100, fax: 444-4094.
A new addition, this is the
hotel at the World Trade

Center, run by Hilton. A
large fitness center, near
to shopping arcades and
free shuttle bus services
to midtown on weekends.

MID-RANGE
Chelsea Hotel,
222 West 23rd Street, tel:
(212) 243-3700, fax: 675-
5531. A hotel with lots of
associations. If you rather
like the idea of staying with
the stars, from the poet,
Dylan Thomas to the punk
star, Sid Vicious, then this
is the place for you.

BUDGET
Washington Square Hotel,
103 Waverly Place,
tel: (212) 777-9515,
fax: 979-8373. Stay right
on the famous square in
Greenwich Village at bargain
rates in this no-frills place.
Good value and all rooms
recently renovated; best
ones have the park view.

Chelsea Center,
511 West 20th,
tel: (212) 643-0214.
It is situated on 10th Avenue
close to the Hudson. Very
low-priced hostel. This offers
communal accommodation
in dormitory style with self-
catering equipment.

WHERE TO EAT

The range of restaurants and
eateries in this city is enormous. From local **bakeries** and
hot dog stands where you

New York City At a Glance

can nibble on snacks as you sightsee, to **chic cafés** and **department store restaurants**, right up the top of the range eateries, there's an awe-inspiring choice. Even the cheap food places are often very good. There are many specialist places from **Jewish dairy cafés** to the delectable parade of **vegetarian restaurants**. There are quite a number of **Indian** places now but it seems that every country in the world is represented in this very food-conscious city with its parade of particular cuisines from **Australia** to **Zambia**. Look out for local fairs and celebrations: some of these such as **Little Italy's festival** are well known but look out for others. It is a lively time when whole neighbourhoods turn out to parade and dance in the streets. During **Restaurant Week**, held in the last week in June, hundreds of establishments offer taster portions and special prix-fixe meals. Also, don't miss the dozens of Chinese restaurants around **Mulberry Street**. Ask for the latest recommendation in a variety of cuisines from the humble **Cantonese** to **Pekingese** and the spicy **Szechwan**. Foodies can go mad at the very thought of New York's incredible range of restaurants, and if you have money to spend, there are some of the leading restaurants in the world to try. Almost all good establishments will take **credit cards**, and New York is a city where hotel restaurants are often of a high standard too.

Midtown
LUXURY
La Côte Basque, 60 West 55th Street, tel: (212) 688-6525. A very smart restaurant serving classic French food. Famous for its evocative murals and a unique style all of its own.

Russian Tea Room, 150 West 57th Street, tel: (212) 974-2111. A grand old New York institution, it is hardly a tearoom, more a kind of Edwardian divan with all sorts of unusual patrons, often theatrical. The food is indeed very Russian, from caviar to crêpes, and you can snack late or have Russian tea with cakes. Cabaret on Sundays. Temporarily closed, check with current restaurant listings for details.

The Four Seasons, 99 East 52nd Street, tel: (212) 754-9494. This is one of the sights of foodie New York, but it's not only famous as a temple to gastronomes, it is very grand and social. The place to try if you want to see smart New York at table.

The Rainbow Room, 230 Rockefeller Plaza, tel: (212) 632-5000. This is a prime place to dine and dance, but it's expensive. Still, with those views from the 65th floor you should lose your head a bit. There's a nightclub too, and if you're not so hungry try the Rainbow Promenade nearby.

MID-RANGE
La Cité, 120 West 51st Street, tel: (212) 956-7100. This restaurant is large and rambling and great for good straightforward food (delicious hamburgers) and big drinks.

Pierre au Tunnel is close to the ever-busy tunnel across to Queens at 250 West 47th Street, tel: (212) 575-1220. The unusual thing about New York is the number of authentic French restaurants, and this is just like an old bistro.

The Palm, Busy and lively at 837 Second Avenue. There is another branch at 840 Second Avenue, tel: (212) 687-2953. If you feel like a steak then this crazy but fun, restaurant is for you. In addition there is lobster and that very New York dish, Clams Casino.

New York City At a Glance

Time, 87 Seventh Avenue South, tel: (212) 220-9100 (there is another in Lafayette Place, tel: (212) 533-7000). Offers basic foods, from pizzas to tapas, as well as special dishes. Friendly and crowded, with nice bar area.

Moto, 328 West 45th Street, tel: (212) 459-9393. Maybe the best Japanese restaurant in town. Smallish menu, very friendly, good value. Evenings only, closed Mondays.

BUDGET
La Fondue, 43 West 55th Street, tel: (212) 581-0820. If cheese is a passion, try this for the all-in-one experience. They also do beef, fish and seafood, so you don't have to eat cheese and afterwards try the chocolate fondue. Low-price, so no credit cards.

Planet Hollywood, 140 West 57th Street, tel: (212) 333-7827. The in place for kids; so much is going on as they eat that the food hardly matters. Expect to wait.

Carmine's, 200 West 44th Street, tel: (212) 221-3800, with a branch uptown at 2450 Broadway at 90th Street. A noisy, friendly, family place with a very New York-Italian atmosphere, open late; home-style food.

Whaler Bar, in the Madison Hotel, tel: (212) 685-3700.

It serves American-style snacks and drinks before a big roaring fireplace in this lofty place. Entertainment is provided. This bar is very popular with locals.

Uptown
LUXURY
Le Cirque 2000, Palace Hotel, 455 Madison Avenue, tel: (212) 794-9292. Fashionable with the well-off and would-be famous. Original food. Reservations are hard to get.

MID-RANGE
Elaine's, 1703 Second Avenue, tel: (212) 534-8103. The sort of personality cult place that only happens in big cities. This is so popular that the food, which is eclectic, doesn't matter.

Kalinka, near the Metropolitan Museum at 1067 Madison Avenue, tel: (212) 564-7112. Appropriately the Russian invasion of New York of the past few years has brought new places to try; this one offers Russian specialities.

Primavera, 1578 First Avenue, tel: (212) 861-8608. This is a quietly-elegant place popular with the locals. Friendly, concerned Italian service.

Mark's, 25 East 77th Street, tel: (212) 879-1864.

A charming in-hotel restaurant off the foyer, offering food all day long in an intimate setting.

BUDGET
American Trash, 1471 First Avenue, tel: (212) 988-9008. As you'd suspect from the name, this is for the kids and there's usually a queue to get in.

Bistro du Nord, 1312 Madison Avenue, tel: (212) 289-0997. A great little French place at East 93rd Street before reaching Spanish Harlem. Warm atmosphere, reasonable French food.

Downtown
MID-RANGE
Katz's Delicatessen Inc, 205 East Houston, tel: (212) 254-2246. This deli caters for older people who enjoy the traditional kosher food.

World Trade Center, 1 World Trade Center, for all restaurants tel: (212) 524-7000, fax: 524-7016. An expensive eatery, called *Windows on the World,* is the top level restaurant. There are other less expensive restaurants here such as **The Greatest Bar on Earth** Hors d'Oeuvrerie (snacks, drinks, dancing) and the **Wild Blue**. The latter is less formal and cheaper, not so high up, yet also offers wide views.

New York City At a Glance

Café Reggio,

119 MacDougal Street, tel: (212) 475-9557. Everything you expect of a village café – dark and a place where unusual people gather. More for snacks than meals. If crowded, try the equally atmospheric Café Dante, 79 MacDougal, tel: (212) 982-5275.

Dean and Deluca Café,

121 Prince Street, tel: (212) 254-8776. Spin-off from the renowned groceries (there's a big one at the roadway corner) in SoHo. A place to snack or have coffee.

Fedora's,

239 West 4th Street, tel: (212) 242-9691. This cosy basement restaurant has been here for decades and offers good food at reasonable prices in a typical atmosphere.

Beyond Manhattan
LUXURY
River Café,

1 Water Street, Brooklyn Heights, tel: (212) (718) 522-5200. Just to show that not all of the expensive places are situated in Manhattan itself, this smart spot cashes in on the view from Brooklyn – near the famous bridge where the one-time barge is moored.

Water's Edge,

44th Drive, Long Island City, tel: (212) (718) 482-0033. Another smart place that takes advantage of Manhattan views. This seafood restaurant is on the city edge of Long Island in Queens, and formal.

MID-RANGE
Henry's End, 44 Henry Street, Brooklyn, tel: (718) 834-1776. Good value and unusual cuisine here – such as kangaroo and elk.

Odessa, 1113 Brighton Beach Avenue, tel: (718) 648-6044. So you want to try the new Russia? Come to Brighton Beach in Brooklyn and try the parade of dishes and the vodka, and the dancing too.

BUDGET
Pastrami King, 124-24 Queens Blvd, tel: (718) 263-1717. New Yorkers get sentimental about where to get good salt beef, or pastrami, and this is a real 'deli' in Queens.

SHOPPING

A place to stretch your legs, in **department stores**, in speciality stores of every kind, in **markets** and even **galleries**. Whatever you require, however much you have to spend, shoppers can find heaven here, and additionally the city is a great fashion

centre. In many countries the dollar exchange rate is good and the amounts of cash you can bring in are considerable. In addition almost every place in New York takes plastic, but check which credit cards are available before you buy. There are great bargains to be found here, particularly in clothes, household goods, gadgets, electrical and computer products, linens, books and CDs. You can even find top labels on sale, (January and other sales are popular times, especially along West 34th Street) or go slumming and sift through stuff on **Orchard Street stalls**. Even thrift shops in the smarter areas can produce good buys and offer fascinating browsing. Try **Chelsea Market** in Union Square for fruit, bread and vegetables. Invaluable for self-caterers. Open Friday and Saturday.

Bookshops are open late and often provide a social hub for like-minded folk, not only for browsers but in their self-contained coffee shops and sitting areas.

Main areas for general shopping are Fifth Avenue from 34th up to 59th, 34th Street, and even the Financial District in Lower Manhattan, or at the vast shopping malls in the boroughs or in New Jersey. These often have branches of top Fifth Avenue shops such as **Saks**, **Bergdorf Goodman** and **Lord and**

New York City At a Glance

Taylor as part of the complex. **FAO Schwarz** is a wonderland of toys for kids at 58th Street. Individual stores in Manhattan, not in mainstream areas, include smart **Bloomingdale's**, the new **Abraham and Strauss** on A & S Plaza, Sixth Avenue and 33rd, and malls such as **Century Plaza**. On newly smart Sixth Avenue below 23rd Street you can shop at **Filene's**, and next door at 18th Street **Old Navy** stocks a selection of trendy sports and casual wear.

Don't overlook **museum shops** – big ones at the Metropolitan and Museum of Modern Art, or whole shopping sections in attractions such as the **South Street Seaport**. If you want to shop but don't have the time, department stores will do it for you with your own **personal shopper** who will discuss your needs and then select items or guide you to specific departments.

If you don't care for big stores, **Madison Avenue** from 42nd Street up has a galaxy of small stylish shops and **East 57th Street** a parade of expensive galleries and boutiques.

Antique shops are all over the Upper East Side with markets like the **Place des Antiquaries** on East 57th, the **Arts and Antique Center** at Second Avenue and East 56th and along Third Avenue.

At the other end of the scale cheap goods can be found along 14th Street, Canal Street, Broadway and in parts of the Lower East Side. Even once exclusive Fifth Avenue in the 40s and 50s has cheap emporiums selling jewellery, carpets and decorative items.

Food shops abound on main avenues like Second, Third and Upper Broadway, but check that foodstuffs can be imported before you leave home. Also be sure that with electrical and software goods you can use them beyond the US. You may need converters or adaptors. Be aware that a sizable sales tax is added to purchases.

TOURS AND EXCURSIONS

From **coach tours** to **walks**, from **helicopter flights** to **cruises** around the harbour, there are lots of possibilities. It's a good idea to check with tourist offices for local trips and ideas. **Circle Lines** take you round the island. Other craft cruise the harbour from the **South Street Seaport** base, or you can even charter your own. The classic harbour cruise is still the one on the Staten Island Ferry and back, but there are also frequent day services out to Liberty and Ellis Islands and once a year Governor's Island is open. Several companies offer Harlem tours with visits to Gospel churches and a typical soul food meal. Beyond

New York try **Greyhound** coach lines or you can rent private cars to be driven out to Connecticut, New Jersey, Long Island and other parts of New York State.

Bicycling
Rent bikes in Central Park at the **Loeb Boathouse**, tel: (212) 861-4137. Other rental places are listed in the commercial section of the New York phone books.

Gray Line of New York
A standard day-long hop-on, hop-off tour or a quick 2-hour introduction is available from 900 Eighth Avenue, for schedules tel: (212) 397-2600.

Shortline Bus Tours
All day or a few hours, a variety available, schedules from 166 West 46th Street, tel: (212) 354-5122.

Trolley Tours
One hour tours in the afternoon, get on and get off as you please at eight stops for a flat fare. The bus is based at South Street Seaport, tel: (212) 677-7268.

Harlem Tours
Harlem Spirituals Inc, 1457, 1697 Broadway, tel: (212) 757-0425 **Harlem Gospel and Jazz Tours**, tel: (212) 302-2594 and **Harlem Renaissance Tours**, tel: (212) 724-9534.

New York City At a Glance

Walking Tours

Many different ones are offered by several organizations around the city. Ask at the information offices for they are often geared to specific areas or interests such as architecture, museums, the community and the arts.

USEFUL CONTACTS

In such a big city you ought to be prepared. New Yorkers are friendly enough, but on the streets they don't always like to talk to strangers, even if they are tourists, so asking questions can be a problem.

Big Apple Greeters: individual volunteers who offer an insider's point of view of New York, tel: (212) 669-2896.

Entertainment Information, a free service updated daily to inform you what's on in New York, 24 hour service, tel: 360-3333. Try also **New York City Onstage** for all arts events, 24 hours, tel: (212) 768-1818. **Theater Tkts** is a booth selling half-price theatre tickets on Times Square, also at 2 World Trade Center. Queue for day of performance tickets for events on and off Broadway.

Post Office: scattered through the city, in each zipcode section, the main one is at Eighth Avenue and 33rd Street.

New York Convention and Visitor's Bureau, 810

Seventh Avenue, NY 10019, tel: (212) 484-1222, fax: 245-5943, website: www.nycvisit.com. For information, not personal visits. For free information and brochures (ask for the *Official NYC Guide*, a pocket-sized quarterly compendium), visit one of the tourist offices situated in the following places: Lobby of the Embassy Theater, 47th and Broadway; Bloomingdale's, Third Avenue; Macy's, 34th Street; Grand Central Terminal; Kennedy Airport. Open every day 09:00-17:00.

Time: to find out the time, tel: (212) 976-1616.
Weather: information on television or in newspapers or tel: (212) 976-1212.

SEX

It may not be advertised as such in brochures and tourist information, but as a city, New York also sells sex. It is available here even though the city authorities continually attempt to 'clean it up'. The girls used to swarm along Eighth Avenue in the 40s, but were moved on when it was decided to give the Theater District a better image. They haven't vanished, though – the girls now solicit cars in Lower Manhattan and around the docks, or in lorry parks in Brooklyn. The crack sellers still crouch in alleys off Eighth Avenue.

Exotically dressed, some of the 'girls' are transvestites. Boys are also available along some avenues and in a number of East and West Side bars. For voyeurs there are sex-cinemas (along midtown Eighth Avenue) with hardcore films. There are live sex shows too, even on Broadway where naked studs strip and strut. In New York anything goes, and liberal laws means that if someone wants it, you can find it here. But take care if you walk or drive through such neighbourhoods as theft and sometimes violence are not uncommon. And it should go without saying, if you do participate take condoms: safe sex is 'de rigueur'.

NEW YORK CITY	J	F	M	A	M	J	J	A	S	O	N	D
AVERAGE TEMP. °C	0	1	5	11	17	22	25	24	20	15	8	2
AVERAGE TEMP. °F	32	33	41	52	62	71	77	75	68	58	47	36
Hours of sun daily	2	3	4	6	7	8	9	8	7	4	3	2
Days of rainfall	12	10	12	11	11	10	12	10	9	9	9	10
RAINFALL mm	94	97	91	81	81	84	107	109	86	89	76	91
RAINFALL in	4	4	4	3.5	3.5	3.5	4	4	3.5	3.5	3	4

Travel Tips

Tourist Information

Cutbacks by Congress have closed the USTTA (US Travel and Tourism Administration) tourist information offices. Currently the private sector is filling the information gap. Travel agents should be able to give the latest news, or try the New York Convention and Visitors Bureau (see page 121 for contact details). In some countries the State of New York may be represented in its own right.

Entry Requirements

You will need a valid passport, but citizens of many countries no longer need a visa to enter, although you can apply for one and then don't need to worry about possible delays on entering. If you have any queries about passports etc contact your local **US Embassy Visa Division** before making plans. Non US residents fill in two forms on arrival and queues form before booths as each entrant is interviewed at the entry point, which can take time.

Customs

Immigration and custom formalities at most airports are now swift and efficient. At some airports sniffer dogs are used to check baggage and they will also indicate if you are carrying fresh fruit, vegetable or meat products. Check beforehand what is not allowed for importation. There are certain duty free allowances to every visitor and US resident so find out before you buy.

Health Requirements

No inoculation certificates are needed, unless you have recently been in an area with an epidemic of cholera, yellow fever, or other contagious sickness. You may be interviewed if you have recently visited a farm in the country you are coming from. If you are taking medication involving drugs, it is wise to have a doctor's letter as proof that you are not bringing in illicit substances. Remember there is very little assistance for health problems in the USA, and treatment is very costly, so along with insurance for

baggage, theft or trip-cancellation costs you should most definitely take out comprehensive medical insurance for the period of your visit.

Getting There

By Air: The airports are within easy reach of the city. There are coach connections to **Grand Central**, the **World Trade Center**, and the **Port Authority (PA)** from **Kennedy** and **LaGuardia**, to the PA from **Newark**. The morning and evening rush hours can lengthen the time taken considerably. There are car rental offices and usually numerous taxis on hand (expensive, and you will have to pay bridge or tunnel tolls). There are few services between midnight and 06:00.
By Rail: The bargain from Kennedy to Midtown Manhattan is the subway which is less than an hour's duration and is a flat fare. Take the free shuttle bus service to the subway station on the airport perimeter (Howard Beach / JFK) and then the fast A train which goes to express stops on the Eighth Avenue

line in Manhattan. Some hotels provide courtesy coaches and there are free shuttle bus services for getting to the various airport terminals. In the planning stages are a Monorail connection to JFK and a Penn Station to Newark rapid shuttle.

By Road: Drive on the right. Roads into Manhattan are major highways, and well marked. Cars pay tolls at most entry points. In the city, roads can be badly deformed and pot-holed: drive carefully. Traffic lights are synchronised along main avenues. Drivers need to carry their licenses and for self-drive cars, full insurance should definitely be considered.

What to Pack

Dress is generally informal, although if you plan to play high stakes and live the smart life of Manhattan you will need fashionable wear, formal gear for good restaurants, including jackets and ties for men and no jeans. Good and comfortable footwear is important, but they don't have to be unattractive, just well broken in. It can be very cold in winter, so pack warm clothes and take gloves and scarves and you may need to get galoshes if it is snowing. This can be a place of extremes, and though New York streets are cleaned quickly, as a rule pavements can be very messy. Take a folding umbrella and rainwear. It is cool and temperate in the short spring and the longer fall, but it can get very hot and

USEFUL PHRASES
elevator • lift
sidewalk • pavement
subway • underground
neat • good
apartment • flat
corn • maize
candy • sweets
nosh • eat
stores • shops
dim sum • chinese dumplings
gumbo • stew
nickel • 5 cents
dime • 10 cents
quarter • 25 cents
buck • dollar

frightfully humid in summer when shorts, blouses or lightweight shirts are necessary. For summer cocktail parties or dinners, however, take lightweight formal wear.

Money Matters

The American dollar (a buck) is the unit and each dollar is divided into 100 cents. Coins are issued in denominations of 1c (called a cent or sometimes a penny) 5c (a nickel), 10c (a dime), 25c (a quarter) 50c and a dollar (dollar coins are not common except in some western states). Notes (paper money) are available in denominations of $1, $2 (rare) $5, $10, $20, $50, $100, $500 and up. Designs of notes are not too different and as the basic colour is the same green you may need to check carefully when paying in cash. Paper money and coins have hardly changed at all except for metal content, which is a bonus as cash or coinage from previous trips will still be

legal tender. The American dollar has fallen against many currencies over the past decade but has stabilized recently.

Currency Exchange: Most currencies are easily exchanged for dollars, and there are no restrictions except that you may not bring more than $10,000 in cash into the USA without making a declaration to Customs. You can take in cash below this limit, or dollar travellers' cheques and exchange money at airport and station booths or at machines taking credit or some bank cards.

Banks: There are some national banks in the USA, and many private ones. Open 09:00 to 15:00. Monday–Friday. Cash machines taking most credit and bank cards are everywhere. Banks will need some form of identification for business other than exchanging cash, such as when changing travellers' cheques. Take a photo ID or a passport. Hotels will change money, though their rates won't necessarily be advantageous. Accredited dealers and travel agents have outlets in main centres, but it's wise to compare exchange rates, especially if cashing large amounts of money.

Credit Cards: The major ones (Visa, Access, American Express, Diners, Delta and Mastercard) are accepted everywhere for many transactions from shopping to petrol. You can also utilize them to get cash. Practically all hotels, restaurants, travel agents and hire companies accept plastic. It is wise however, to take out an insurance policy against theft on all your credit cards.

Tipping: Regardless of the quality of service (or lack of it) most people add 15% to restaurant and bar bills, taxi-fares and services from hotel room staff. Beware the wrath of some drivers, porters or waiters untipped in certain restaurants. Porters often have a fixed rate. When checking out remember there will be City and State taxes added to your bill (also on shopping and for meals).

Gambling: You can gamble in many ways in New York. Popular are horse and surrey racing, results of box-ing or wrestling matches and other sports. There are casi-nos at some major hotels.

Accommodation

A vast range of prices from the most luxurious and expensive hotels in the world to simple motels on the West Side or even bed-and-breakfasts. And for students and the budget-minded there are plain down-to-earth dormitory hos-tels. You can book ahead using services or there are booking facilities for hotels at the airports and stations.

Eating Out

You are spoiled for choice in New York. Every kind of food is available from the best of the Parisian style and New York cooking to soul food. Many snack bars offer sand-wiches – some New York favourites such as pastrami salt

beef and of course, big ham-burgers are bargains. Pretzels and bagels are typical snacks. Steak houses offer grilled meats and salads at competi-tion prices. Local restaurants have special offers, big sand-wiches and rich desserts.

Transport

New York has a well-developed, reasonable public transport system. The subway is extensive, covering four boroughs (and one line on Staten Island). It operates 24 hours a day on a flat fare for the Central area. Bus services on main avenue and cross streets at flat fare, sometimes transfers to and from subways are possible. New York is a terminus for many airlines and trains. Coaches and trains provide airport connections to Grand Central Terminal and the Port Authority.

Women Travellers: There are many precautions that need to be considered in a city like New York where a woman often feels unsafe when alone. It is important to appear confi-dent and alert when out in the city. It's wise to prepare beforehand with books and

information on women's services or accommodation. Plan to go straight to the information offices and ask about sensible ways to operate in the city.

Business Hours

Americans seem to work longer and longer hours, and New York is no exception with the bizarre 'power breakfasts' starting as early as 06:30. Business, however, doesn't get geared up at most offices until 08:30 or 09:00 and goes on often without lunch breaks to 17:30 or 18:00, Monday–Friday. Banks are open from 09:00–15:00, but many have 24 hour automatic cash machines (you may need to swipe a bank or credit card to enter the space). Shops and supermarkets stay open later on most evenings (Thursday shopping to 21:00 at depart-ment stores) and are also open on Sundays. Some foodstores serve customers past midnight. Fruit, veg and food stalls, espe-cially along the lower East Side avenues, are open all night as are some cafés and snack bars, which even if they are

CONVERSION CHART		
FROM	**TO**	**MULTIPLY BY**
Millimetres	Inches	0.0394
Metres	Yards	1.0936
Metres	Feet	3.281
Kilometres	Miles	0.6214
Kilometres square	Square miles	0.386
Hectares	Acres	2.471
Litres	Pints	1.760
Kilograms	Pounds	2.205
Tonnes	Tons	0.984
To convert Celsius to Fahrenheit: x 9 ÷ 5 + 32		

not 24-hour operations, start early and close late. Many bars of which there is a great variety in New York, are open all day and often only close for a couple of hours at night, usually from 04:00–06:00 to clean up. Big hotels will have round the clock reception and room service facilities.

Time Difference
New York is five hours behind GMT, and puts its clocks forward for one hour during summer time.

Communications
Telecommunications: Public telephones in the city are run by several companies. Numbers consist of a three digit code and seven digit numbers. In Manhattan it is not necessary to add the code, but the other boroughs will require it. Long distance calls require a 1 before the ten digits. 800 calls are toll-free numbers, 900 numbers are definitely not, and they can be costly. Directory assistance for local calls is 411, for long distance dial 555 1212 prefixing with the usual 1 and the area code. You can make person-to-person or collect calls or pay with coins, using public phones, but as this can mean a large handful of loose change for calls made through the operator from public phones it's best to buy a telephone card, or use any one of several credit cards. **Help Lines:** There are a number of help telephone lines to assist you. **The Yellow Pages**

list agencies and counselling aids, or the **Talking Yellowbook** on (212) 718 921-1400, suggests needs and then gives code numbers for local information for the cost of a local call. **Postal services:** Post offices are based at each zip code area of the city, with the main one at 34th Street and 8th Avenue being **New York 10001**. (The whole country has five digit codes, and to speed delivery sometimes there is an additional four digit number attached). Postage varies from postcards to local mail and if you need special stamps there is sometimes a particular counter. All services are offered plus copying and fax in most offices. If you require to receive mail tell correspondents to send letters allowing plenty of delivery time, c/o General Delivery at New York City, NY addressed to the specific zip code of the office at which you wish to pick up mail. Post offices are open from 08:00–17:00 and from 08:00 to midday on Saturdays. Closed on all public holidays.

Electricity
The system uses 110-120 volts 60 cycles in the USA. The plugs are two-pin, so when buying a necessary current converter ensure it will work in the US.

Weights and Measures
The USA consistently refuses to go metric, unlike Canada, and abides by the old British system of measuring in feet,

PUBLIC HOLIDAYS
January 1 • New Year's Day
January 15 • Martin Luther King Day
3rd Monday in May • Presidents' Day
Last Monday in May • Memorial Day
July 4th • Independence Day
1st Monday in September • Labour Day
November 11 • Veterans Day
Last Thursday in November • Thanksgiving Day
December 25 • Christmas Day

yards and miles. For weights they use pounds and ounces and the regular gallon (not the imperial) and pints for liquids. People have little idea of metric equivalents so if buying shoes, clothes or fabrics you may need to convert. Temperatures are measured in **Fahrenheit**.

Health Precautions
Do not even think of going to New York without taking adequate medical insurance. Buy it for the trip, as part of a regular insurance policy, or at the last minute where it can be purchased at some airports. It could cost a fortune for anyone unlucky enough to fall ill here without coverage, for though hospitals are right up to date they are very costly places to stay in. There are some free hospitals ('charity' ones) but they are crowded and overworked and often understaffed. You can

be referred to a private hospital by a general practitioner. In an emergency go direct to a casualty ward, where they will usually want proof that you can pay your bill before offering services (often a recognized credit card imprint suffices).

Health Services

Very minimal unless you are prepared to pay substantially. New York has the finest hospitals and clinics, but you'll need a credit card. It's imperative to take out health insurance for a visit here.

Personal Safety

It's sensible not to look like a tourist. Try and avoid the obvious clothes and appendages such as camera bags. And most importantly for women, conceal or don't wear jewellery. Keep your wallet or purse in one pocket and have ready money in another, or wear one of those unattractive yet useful money belts. Take only what you need, maybe concealing an extra note somewhere about your person, although muggers have been known to check inside shoes. Carry at least one, preferably two, forms of identification. On the streets, walk as if you know where you are going, dawdling and too much 'rubber-necking' can mark you out. Avoid poor and dangerous areas, and at night don't walk in parks. Don't get caught up with con artists – there are lots of them in the city, operating

all sorts of tricks. Hustlers are common in certain areas such as the **Pennsylvania Station**. Ask directions from policemen or doormen or BIDs, or go into shops or cafés. Never leave anything that looks valuable and that can be seen in a car. If you are travelling at night it's preferable to use surface transport but if there is no bus, then stay near subway token booths until the train arrives. Some stations will have a posse of the so-called **Guardian Angels** on hand in their red berets to ensure safety. Late at night the safest form of transport is a taxi.

Senior Citizens: If you are taking medication, or may need assistance, remember to keep a note to that effect on your person in order to pass on the information to a helper.

Emergencies
Embassies and Consulates: New York has a large representation of consulates, listed in the telephone book. If you require assistance from your embassy, you may need to contact the capital, Washington. There are UN missions from most countries based in New York.

Etiquette

New Yorkers are not truly Americans – much as Berliners are not German. New York is a state of mind as well as a great city. The residents are proud of being New Yorkers and don't care for undue criticism from anybody. Many

places in the city are strictly non-smoking. Smokers should check before lighting up.

Language

English is spoken everywhere in the USA, but in some neighbourhoods you will still hear a European tongue or even Yiddish. Almost everyone understands and speaks English, but in some cities, notably New York and Miami, **Spanish** is very much a major second language. The influx of Mexicans has made Spanish a second language in LA, but it is mostly due to the Puerto Rican influx in NY City that large numbers of the population hardly use English at all.The arrival of new Caribbean and South American settlers has brought French and Portuguese into the mix. You might have a French-speaking Haitian as a cab driver!

GOOD READING

While you are in New York City, don't forget to get hold of a copy of The New York Times or Village Voice for news and information on current events. There are also several magazines, such as The New Yorker and the New York Magazine, which are very interesting and filled with helpful information.
• Morrone, Francis, The Architectural Guidebook to New York City (Gibbs-Smith).
• Alleman, Richard, The Movie Lover's Guide to New York (Harper & Row).

INDEX

accommodation 114,
    115, 116, 124
Aids Memorial **98**
Albany 6, 111
Algonquin Indians 9, 11, 14
Algonquin Hotel 23
Alice Tully Hall 91
Alphabet City **41**
Amagansett 5, 107
American Civil War 14, 15
American Craft Museum 76
American Football 26
American Museum of
    Natural History 87,
    89, 92
Apollo Theater 24, 96
Aqueduct Race Track 103
Art Deco 23, **24**, 25, 35,
    67, 71, 72, 75, 83, 93
Astor Place 52
Atlantic City **109**
Audubon Terrace 96
Aunt Len's Doll and Toy
    Museum 96
Avenue of the Arts 10
Avery Fisher Hall 24, 91

Balanchine, George 24
Bank of Manhattan 62
Barnard College 95, 98
Bartholdi, Frédéric 32
baseball **26**
basketball 26
Battery, The 9, 31, 32,
    34, 37
Bayard Building 42
Bear Mountain 111
Belvedere Castle 82
Bethesda Fountain 82
Bloomingdale's 14, 68, **84**
Boricua College 96
Boss Tweed 12
Bowery, The 39, 42, 44, 45
Brighton Beach 107
British Museum 85
Broadway 9, 10, 22, 23,
    25, 35, 44, 45, 47, 50,
    53, 55, 60, 61, 65, 74,
    89, 91
Bronx, The 5, 7, 26
Bronx Zoo 7, 87, **104**
Brooklyn 5, 7, 10, 26,
    102, 103
Brooklyn Battery Tunnel
    102

Brooklyn Botanical Garden
    102, 103
Brooklyn Bridge 14, 15, **37**
Brooklyn Heights 32, 102
buskers **20**
Butler Library 98

Canal Street 39, 40, 53, 56
Cape May 109
Caribbean Islands 39
Carnegie Hall 15, **24**, 72
Castle Clinton 32
Castro, Fidel 96
Cathedral of St John the
    Divine 14, 21, 95, 98
Cather, Willa 23
Catskill Mountains 111
Central Park 5, 6, 7, 8, 10,
    14, 15, 20, 21, 26, **81**,
    82, 83, 87, **92**
Chagall 76, 85
Chanin Building 65, 72
Charles II 12
Chelsea 10, 25, 59, 62
Chelsea Hotel 23, 59, **62**
Children's Museum of
    Manhattan 93, 104
Chinatown 28, 36, **39**, 42,
    43, **44**
Chinese New Year 40
Christopher Street **49**, 51,
    52, 53
Chrysler building **16**, 25,
    62, 65, 71
Church of the
    Incarnation 72
City Hall 36
Civic Center 31, 36
climate 7, 113, 121
Cloisters, The 95, 99
Colonnade, The 46
Columbia University 12,
    95, 98
Columbus Circle 93
Columbus Day Parade 21
Connecticut 101, 110
Cooper, Peter 46
Cooper Union 39, 45, 46
Cotton Club 96, 97
Coward, Noël 16
Cuba 21, 28
Cushman Row 62
customs 122

Daily News Building 72
Dakota Apartments 92
De Kooning 87
Delacorte Theater 83
Dinkins, Mayor 18

Dutch West Indies
    Company 11
Dutch settlers 9, 11, 12,
    14, 31, 35

East Houston Street 39, 41
East River 6, 7
East Village 25, **45**
Easthampton 5
eating out 116, 117, 118,
    119, 124
Eighth Avenue 27
El Barrio 96, 97
Ellis Island 14, 15, 31,
    32, 33
Empire State Building 5,
    10, 14, 16, 18, 25, 59,
    62, **65**
Erie Canal 13, 14
Essex House 25, 27, 73

FAO Schwarz 73
Federal Hall National
    Monument 35
Federal Reserve Bank 35
Fifth Avenue 5, 9, 10, 50,
    52, 61, 63, 65, 72, 73,
    74, 78, 81, **83**, 85, 90,
    97, 99
Financial District 9, 13, 17,
    25, 28, 31, 36, 56
Finger Lakes 111
Fire Island 5, 106, 107
Flatiron Building 59, 61, 62
Ford Foundation 72
Fordham University 89
Fort Tryon Park 95, 99
Fort Washington Park 99
Fort Williams 32
Four Seasons Restaurant
    27, 77
Fraunces Tavern 31, 34
Frick Collection 74, 81, 86
Fuller Building 59, 77
Fulton Fish Market 37

Garment District 65, 66
General Electric Building 77
George Washington Bridge
    95, 108
Giants' Stadium 26
Giuliani, Mayor 18
Goethe–Institut 84
Grace Church 47
Gramercy Park 59, 62, **63**
Grand Central Station 25,
    65, **71**, 81
Great Depression 14, 16,
    17, 67

Greenwich Village 5, 9,
    10, 13, 19, 22, 45, 49,
    51, 54
Guggenheim Museum 85
Gulf War 18

Hamilton Grange 96
Hamptons, The 107
Harlem 7, 10, 13, 14, 19,
    95, 96
Harlem Third World
    Trade Center 96
Hartford 110
Harvard Club 63
Haughwort Building 55
Hayden Planetarium 87,
    89, 92
Hispanics 20, 21, 39
history 11–17
Holliday, Billy 97
hotels 114, 115, 116
Houston Street 40, 50
Hudson River 5, 6, 14, 16,
    50, **53**, 99, **111**
Hudson, Henry 14
Hyde Park 111

immigrants 14, 15, 20, 33
International Center of
    Photography 84
International Wildlife
    Conservation Center 8

Jacob K Javits Conference
    Center 68
Jacques Marchais Center
    of Tibetan Art 105
James, Henry 23, 52
Jefferson Market
    Courthouse 52, 53
Jewish Lower East Side 39
Jewish Museum 84
Judson Memorial Church 52
Juilliard School 24, 89

Kennedy Airport 102, 103
Kennedy, John F **18**
King, Martin Luther 18
Knickerbockers 26
Koch, Ed 15, 18

Lafayette Place 46
Lafayette Street 39
LaGuardia Airport 103
LaGuardia, Fiorello 14,
    16, 18
Lake Champlain 111
Lambertville 109
Lever Building 17

Lexington Avenue 63
Lincoln Center 5, 14, 17,
    24, 53, 89, 90, **91**
Lind, Jenny 32
Litchfield **110**
Little Italy 22, 28, 39, 42, 43
Little Red Lighthouse **99**
Little Russia 107
Long Island 5, 7, 27, 101,
    106, 107, 109
Lord and Taylor's 73
Lower East Side 13, 15, 35,
    40, 41, 42, 43, 45

MacDougal Street 51
Macy's 65, **68**, 69
Madison Avenue 73, 83
Madison Square Garden
    24, 25, 26, 59, 61, 67
Manhattan 5, 6, 7, 9, 13,
    14, 17, 19, 29, 31, 32,
    33, 34, 65, 72
Manhattan Antique
    Center 73
Marble Collegiate
    Church 72
Mark Hotel 27
Metropolitan Museum of Art
    15, **22**, 81, 83, 85, **86**
Metropolitan Opera House
    90, **91**
Midtown 5, 10, 13, 19, 22,
    25, 59, 63, 65, 91
Millennium Hotel 27
Mills Mansion 111
Moore, Clement 62
More, Thomas **87**
Morningside Park 95, 98
Mott Street 44
Mulberry Street 43
Murray Hill 70
Museo del Barrio 84, 97
Museum of American
    Constitutional
    Government 34
Museum of Chinese in the
    Americas 45
Museum of Jewish Heritage
    34
Museum of Modern Art
    22, 65, **76**
Museum of the American
    Indian 34
Museum of the City
    of New York 84

National Academy
    of Design 84
New Amsterdam 11, 12

New England 110
New Haven 110
New Hope 109
New Jersey 5, 26, 42, 53,
    56, 101, 108
New London 110
New York Aquarium
    32, 103, 107
New York Botanical
    Gardens 7, 104
New York Historical
    Society 93
New York Public Library 15,
    65, **69**
New York State Theater
    24, 91
New York Stock
    Exchange 35
New York University 52
Newhouse Center 104
Newport 110
Nureyev, Rudolf 92

Off-Broadway 23, 50
O'Keeffe 87
Old Colony Club 63
Old Docks, The 37, 54
Old Merchant's House 46
Olmsted, Frederick Law
    82, 93, 99
O'Neill, Eugene 110
One Wall Street 35
Orchard Street 39, **41**
Oyster Bar 27

Pan Am Building 72
Paramount Hotel 27
Park Avenue 65, 83
Parker, Charlie 97
Pennsylvania Station
    25, 67, 106
Picasso 76, 85
Pierpont Morgan Library
    65, 70
Place des Antiquaires 73
Plaza 73, 78
Poe, Edgar Allan 50
Pollock 87
Princeton 101, 108
Prohibition 14, 96
Puck Building 42

Quakers 11, 103
Queens 5, 7, 102, 103

Radio City Music Hall
    23, 25, **75**
restaurants 116–119
Rhode Island 110

Richmond 5, **105**
Riverside Park 89, 93
Riverside Church **89**
Rockefeller Center 7, 16,
    25, 65, 74, 75, 78

São Paulo 20
St Mark's in the Bowery 45
St Mark's Place **9**, 47
St Patrick's Cathedral
    21, 74, **79**
St Paul's Chapel 35
Saks 73
San Francisco 22, 28,
    40, 42, 43
Schermerhorn Row 37
Seagram Building 5, 17, 77
Seaport Liberty Cruise 37
Shea Stadium 24, 26, 103
shopping 119
Siegal-Cooper 63
slavery 14, 95
Smithsonian Institute 34
Snug Harbour 104, 105
SoHo 5, 10, 22, 49, **54**, 57
South Street Seaport
    31, **36**, **111**
Spanish Harlem 19, 81, 95
Spanish Museum 97
Staten Island 5, 7, 32, 33,
    101, 105
Staten Island Ferry 31, 33,
    55
Statue of Liberty 5, 14, 15,
    31, 32, 33
Stock Market Crash 14
Stonecutting Yard 98
Stonewall Riots 53
Strand Book Store 52, 90
Striver's Row 96
Stuyvesant, Peter **11**, 14,
    45, 103
Symphony Space 93

Tammany Hall 12
TKTS (Theater tickets)
    Booth 23, **25**, 74
Temple Emmanu-El 87
Theater District 13, 27
Theodore Roosevelt's
    Birthplace 63
Theological Seminary 62
Tiffany's **73**
Times Square 23, 65, **74**
Tompkins Square Park 47
tourist information centres
    121, 122
tours 120, 121
transport 113, 114

travel tips 122–126
Triangle Shirtwaist
    Factory 15
TriBeCa 10, 22, 49, 56, 57
Trinity Church 35
Trump Tower **9**, 78
Twain, Mark 110
Tweed Courthouse 36

Union Square 59, 60, 61
United Nations Building
    17, **70**
United States Custom
    House 34
University Club 63
Upper Broadway 23
Upper East Side 10, 19,
    62, 81
Upper West Side 10, 13,
    22, 23, 89, 90

Van Cortland Mansion 104
Vanderbilt Mansion 111
Van Gogh 85
Vaux, Calvert 82
Vermeer 86
Verrazano, Giovanni de 14
Victory Theater 15
Vivian Beaumont Theater 91

Waldorf-Astoria 25, **78**
Walker, Jimmy 16
Wall Street 9, 16, 35
War of Independence
    12, 14, 34, 99
Warhol, Andy 87
Washington, George **12**,
    34, 35, 52, 104
Washington Heights 10,
    95, 99
Washington Square 49,
    52, 53,
West Point Military
    Academy 111
Wharton, Edith 23
Whitney Museum 34, 81, 87
Winter Garden 34
Woolworth Building 10
World Financial Center 34
World Trade Center 14, **19**,
    31, 34, 35, 62
World Trade Towers 17
Wright, Frank Lloyd 85
Wright, Wilbur 14

Yale 110
Yiddish 21

Zabar's 93